Teaching Ideas for
the Come-Alive Classroom

Dorothy Zjawin

Teaching Ideas for the Come-Alive Classroom

Parker Publishing Company, Inc.
West Nyack, New York

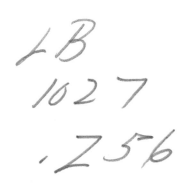

LB
1027
.Z56

© 1980 by

PARKER PUBLISHING COMPANY, INC.

West Nyack, N.Y.

All rights reserved. No part of this
book may be reproduced in any form or
by any means, without permission in
writing from the publisher.

DISCARDED

WIDENER COLLEGE
WOLFGRAM
LIBRARY
CHESTER, PA.

WIDENER UNIVERSITY

Library of Congress Cataloging in Publication Data

Zjawin, Dorothy
   Teaching ideas for the come-alive classroom.

   Includes bibliographies and index.
   1. Activity programs in education.   2. Teaching—
Aids and devices.   I. Title.
LB1027.Z56   372.13   80-15209
ISBN 0-13-893446-0

Printed in the United States of America

HOW THIS BOOK WILL HELP YOU MAKE YOUR CLASSROOM COME ALIVE

You do not need a bag of miracles to turn children on to the excitement of learning. Often, the simplest approaches when used properly (and creatively) are most effective. To motivate a child to think, first provide the opportunity to think, along with a good reason or some form of stimulus that will cause the child to *apply* that thinking. This can best be done when you add a spark of excitement to the classroom. And that is what this book is all about.

During many years in teaching, I have found that simplicity is the best prelude to the development of an effective learning aid. For example, to add a lively element to social history and pave the way for a study of the Revolutionary War, you can excite and interest the class with a discussion of how Colonial children worked and played. As another example, you'll be amazed at how investigating the childhood of King Tut will work wonders when you present some of the invaluable lessons learned from Ancient Egypt. Other intriguing approaches in this book include a lesson plan on "Stonehenge As an Ancient Mystery" and "What the Future Will Be Like."

As you begin to realize the diversity of the hundreds of ideas in this book, you will discover many ways, for example, to improve language skills by the simple device of using art. A good art activity will often help you motivate even the most reluctant learner. When it is combined with unique ways to increase reading skills via "story centers," however, art can also prompt pupils to discuss projects, follow instructions, inspire them with ideas for any number of creative learning activities, plus enable them to use research skills to find out what was really in that legend. The possibilities are infinite.

As another indication of this book's practical value, in one section of Chapter 4 you will find math problems—other than the storybook kind—that provide intriguing challenges to stimulate thinking. Cubes and Soma puzzles, rather than the traditional devices, are some of the tools used for active problem solving.

Still other chapters include a delightful assortment of ways to perk up your class during those dreary weeks after the holidays. No longer will the days between early January and the end of February seem tiresome and unproductive. As long as you can take advantage of the "Special Days" in between, you and your class will have lots to look forward to. In addition, the holidays themselves will take on special meaning when you apply the ideas offered in Chapter 3.

Every chapter overflows with tried and proven activities, games, motivators and lesson plans that will help you create and maintain a "Come-Alive Classroom." The children will become your delighted allies instead of mere students, for example, just by applying the ideas in Chapter 2, which is devoted to ways of helping pupils think creatively. Yet another example of this book's usefulness is in Chapter 3, which helps you put your own creativity to work in making the most of classroom "communications aids" on short notice. As you are well aware, even the simplest device such as the classroom bulletin board takes time to prepare and implement. How many times have you wished that you had time to change those boards more often to really increase their value? This chapter shows you how. It offers a bonanza of hints that will help you build classroom communications around interesting, thought-provoking themes. There are even five ready-made bulletin boards you can use immediately.

So, when you need ideas to begin a new topic, ways to add spark or vitality, and the kind of lesson plan that will cause a surge of excitement in your classroom, you'll find them in this book.

Read on, apply, and most of all, *enjoy* the exhilaration that comes when you realize you have achieved the "Come-Alive Classroom."

Dorothy Zjawin

CONTENTS

Contents

8. EXPLORING THE PRESENT SCENE AND
   TOMORROW *(Cont'd.)*

10. PRACTICAL LISTING METHODS THAT
    MEASURE PROGRESS *(Cont'd.)*

Teaching Ideas for
the Come-Alive Classroom

1

ESTABLISHING THE COME-ALIVE CLASSROOM —THE EASY WAY

By starting with a familiar item or two, you can increase and enhance children's learning. And what could be more familiar to a child than his or her own name? Or taking an item like an egg carton and transforming it into an attractive learning aid? Or better still, introducing a primary math lesson with nothing more than a paper bag and a few empty juice containers?

As you might have guessed, reading and math basics can also be included, for your pupils will have more opportunities to practice these and other subject skills as well. To begin with, take a look at what can be done with names—pupils' names, nicknames, *and* those of famous people. Immediately following these suggestions are ways to use other things children may be familiar with and interested in. For more ideas, check the alphabetized list of throwaway sources that can be collected and put to work as soon as you like.

ACTIVITIES WITH PUPILS' NAMES

1. Print each child's name on a separate strip of construction paper, about 2 × 6 inches. Scatter these strips randomly on a large desk, table or floor. Then give each child a turn to find his "name strip" on the desk or table, and read it. Pupils who read their names correctly may keep their "strip."

2. Instead of assigning class jobs in the usual way, choose pupils whose first names begin with a certain letter, such as "J" for "John" and "Jean."

3. Play "Name Bingo." Print names on blank bingo cards and play the game in the usual way, or have pupils make up their own versions.

4. Have younger pupils make up their own special name tags. Use yarn, rope, and other scrap materials to spell out names.

5. Older students might enjoy looking up the lives of recent celebrities or historical personalities with the same first name. These findings may be recorded in a booklet or other project.

6. Have older (or more able) pupils investigate the origins of their names. If possible, children may also learn how their first names "look" in a foreign language. What differences are there?

7. Ask children to choose a different name for themselves and write what they would do and how they would live with their new identities.

8. Nicknames provide a good topic for discussion and/or debate. How did nicknames begin in the first place? How do pupils feel about their own or someone else's nickname? Why?

9. If the class is studying American history, some children may be interested in investigating what kind of names people had at that particular time.

10. What is an alias? Have pupils give examples, such as "Clark Kent" for "Superman."

While children's names make effective teaching aids, they are by no means the only materials you can use to personalize the curriculum. The following suggestions may be used as "starting points" to focus on the children in your class.

1. Use this activity in an appropriate science unit or lesson. On a 8½ × 11-inch piece of colored posterboard,

glue a mirror on the top half and write directions as shown in Figure 1-1.

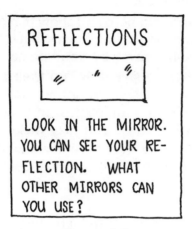

Figure 1-1

2. Remember that children's special heroes and heroines, birthdays, pets, ethnic backgrounds and hobbies make good starting points for language, social studies, science and math lessons. Examples of how to extend these topics are listed below.

Suggestions for Using Special Heroes and Heroines, Birthdays, Pets & Other Topics

Take a class poll of heroes and heroines in "real life" and fiction. Ask each child to write down his or her favorite personality on a slip of paper and use the results of this survey to:

- Make a directory of heroes and heroines.
- Find out more about the era and place where the hero or heroine lived, worked, and played.
- Make up myths, plays, or stories about these special people. Try using different settings and/or times.
- Take this opportunity to explore some of the older myths, such as those of the ancient Greeks and Romans, and compare them to their modern counterparts.

- Pick out a stereotyped hero and give him or her new qualities and/or shortcomings. Include him or her in a set of new adventures.
- Make up a modern hero and show him or her overcoming some of our nation's problems. What is his (or her) name? Is this person known by another name to friends and acquaintances? Does this name tell anything about him or her?
- Explore derivations of names and nicknames of other heroes and heroines. You may include the example of Richard the Lion-Hearted. (Who was he? When did he live? Was he liked by people?)

Birthdays

- Encourage older pupils to learn what happened the year they were born. Who was President at that time? What new conveniences did people have or were they about to get? What kind of music was popular? What other famous personalities lived at the time? What did their neighborhood look like then? What did some of the headlines in the newspapers say?

Pets

- Make up silly pets similar to "pet rock." Try drawing them first, then make models in clay or papier-mâché.
- Collect stories about people who own unusual pets.
- Make posters for "Be Kind to Animals Week."
- Children might find it interesting to consider what the first dogs and cats might have looked like, and to make up stories, Kipling-style, about the first dog or cat to become someone's pet.
- Read to learn why ancient peoples thought certain animals were important enough to be worshipped. What were the legends behind these so-called "gods"?
- Try classifying animals as the scientists do. First draw a picture of different animals on separate 3 × 5-inch cards.

Try for as much variety as possible by including those animals that walk, fly and crawl, as well as animals with bills, scales, fur and feathers.

Ethnic Backgrounds

- Find out what a "typical day" is like for a foreign child and compare it to one of your students' days.
- Make dolls of various nationalities, placing them in their native settings. To do this, cut down a shoe box or cardboard carton as shown; then tape or place the doll inside. (See Figure 1-2.)

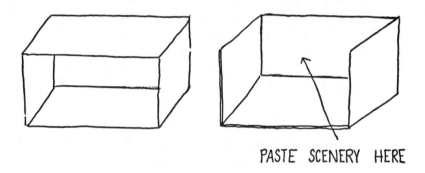

PASTE SCENERY HERE

Figure 1-2

- Investigate stereotypes associated with some nationalities and compare them with facts. For example, Dutch people dress very much like we do. Even in the country, wooden shoes are the exception, not the rule.
- Find out how a well-known holiday like Christmas is celebrated in other lands.
- Learn the words to a popular song in a foreign language.

Hobbies

- In addition to having history, current events, and geography in common, *stamp* and *coin collecting* also involve math. How much does a foreign coin or stamp "cost" in our money? What is its worth in foreign money? If it's

worth X amount of dollars, you are able to sell it for
_____ in foreign currency.

- Black and white photographs of familiar subjects can be
used to motivate children to attempt their own similar
pictures and designs. Have them experiment with any or
all of the following activities:
    1. Simplify background scenes and use them with
    shadow puppets and/or silhouettes.

    2. Using black and white crayons, paper pieces, or
    newspaper pieces, create a similar scene or design
    on white or black paper.

- Enrich those *drawing* and *painting* projects by collecting
pictures of well-known and not so well-known artists'
renditions of flowers, animals, portraits, buildings, city
scenes, and so on. Have children look for and think of
how art can be used to beautify their city or immediate
neighborhood.

Gardening

- Look at as many seed catalogs as you and the children can
obtain. Make up arithmetic problems that compare the
costs and savings on various brands of seeds.

- Learn how to make paper flowers. When you have different kinds, try putting on a class flower show. This
might make a good "Welcome Spring" activity.

- Identify certain flowers by looking at their scientific
names and their meanings. If possible, check out any
connected legends or stories.

- Make flower pendants from clean jar tops. First cut or
draw a picture of a flower and paste it on a jar top. Before
covering this pendant with cellophane or shellac, punch a
hole at the top for a string.

- Find out about scarecrows in fact and fiction.

- Make up poems about gardens and gardeners.

- Draw pictures of garden scenes found in various stories
such as *Peter Rabbit, Alice in Wonderland,* and *Jack and
the Beanstalk.*

- Paste pictures of flowers on 3 × 5-inch cards, place this deck of cards face down, and try to identify each card as it is picked up.
- Gardens were often laid out in geometric patterns and designs. Using pictures from various seed catalogs and magazines, design your own garden. Cut out pictures of shrubs, flowers and trees, and put them in a design on a piece of paper.

Cars

- Find pictures, make models of old cars, and investigate the time during which they were made.
- Taking the energy crisis into consideration, design the car of the future.
- Learn to read road maps and take note of the symbols used to depict railroads, highways and landmarks.
- Find out about vehicles other than cars, such as racing cars and vans.
- What occupations are associated with the automobile industry? Pretend you are interested in applying for one of them. In your letter of application, explain why you think you would be qualified for this job.
- Learn about road safety, street signs, and symbols.
- Find out the code used in CB language which denotes certain words, such as "help." Try writing a message to a friend using CB terms and see if he can "read" it. Investigate other types of codes.
- Draw the kind of design or picture you would use to decorate a van.

TEN TIMESAVERS TO USE ON OR BEFORE THE FIRST DAY OF SCHOOL

1. If possible, bring a Polaroid® camera to take pupils' pictures and use these pictures, with the child's name under each in a "Welcome Back!" bulletin board.
2. Place a large piece of cork nearby as a catchall for memos and other items that can easily be replaced.

3. Mimeograph plenty of copies of blank seating charts and class roster sheets. Include a completed copy of each in the folder for substitute teachers.

4. Have a wide variety of things to do for pupils who complete work early. Look in childrens' activity books for ideas. While you are at it, look for and include reading and math activities suitable for a wide range of abilities. For easier handling, place similar activities in designated envelopes and tape these envelopes near the blackboard and/or bulletin boards.

5. Although the middle of the school year sounds like it's a long way off, it will be here before you know it. For the time being, overlook the holiday months of November, December and April, and make plans for the months ahead. In your planning, keep in mind the question "What can I do to make children look forward to that first week in May or June?"

6. Begin now to make rough sketches of possible bulletin boards for September and October. If possible, prepare lettering and pictures to be used with these boards.

7. Keep an extra notebook to hold alternative and/or "spur-of-the-moment" plans.

8. Prepare a different substitute folder—this time with pockets! Glue or tape the class roster and seating chart inside and place sheets with alternate activities and extra suggestions for an educational game or two inside. You can encourage your substitute to leave ideas and/or plans which she has found useful, particularly in lauguage arts and math. An example of a substitute folder is shown in Figure 1-3.

9. Instead of labeling containers "Pencils," "Crayons" and "Brushes," go one step further and include simple directions, such as "Put broken pencils in here." (See Figure 1-4.)

10. Review "how to study" methods with pupils by covering such aspects as note-taking, outlining and finding a

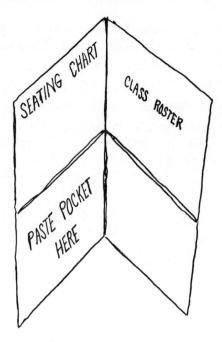

Figure 1-3

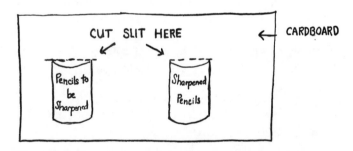

Figure 1-4

book in the library. Use the following suggestions to help pupils make their work easier:

- In taking notes in social studies, science, and similar subjects, try to answer the questions "Who," "What," "Where," "Why" and "When" as briefly as possible.

- Learn to abbreviate certain words such as "and," "history," "department" and so on.
- Instead of a large explanation, try substituting a picture with appropriate labels.
- In math, find out *how* a solution was reached.
- Not all outlines need full details, especially if you plan to study from them. Instead, shorten headings to include only key words. For example, try "Causes of Rev. War" instead of "The Causes of the Revolutionary War."
- To help save time, find the same book by its title *or* its author in the library's card catalog.
- To help the librarian help *you*, say, "I am looking for a book (magazine or newspaper) that tells something about how the ancient Egyptians lived," instead of, "I want a book about Egypt." In other words, say exactly what you are interested in to the best of your ability.
- On index cards, write important math and science formulas that you use often. That way, you will be able to refer to them quickly and easily.

DEVELOPING TREASURES FROM 50 EASY-TO-OBTAIN SCRAP MATERIALS

1. *Advertisements* can be cut out, mounted on 8½ × 11-inch sheets of construction paper and used for activity cards. See in Figure 1-5.

2. *Buttons, bottle caps,* and *blocks* make good counters and game pieces/markers.

3. *Calendars* may be cut apart and used to reinforce number skills. For example, cut out separate number "squares" from calendar pages, mount (paste) them on cardboard, cut out and you have an instant learning aid! Pupils can place these number "squares" in numerical order, match them with other numbered squares or corresponding numbers of toys, and fill in

spaces on cards made for this purpose. Examples are shown in Figure 1-6.

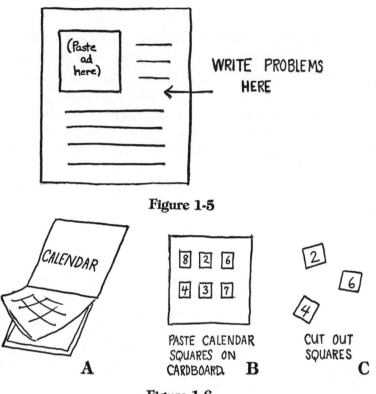

Figure 1-5

Figure 1-6

4. *Cancelled stamps* also provide other opportunities for number work as well as different learning experiences in social studies and art.
   - Through stamps, children can be motivated to learn more about a certain invention, famous personality, or "hot" environmental issues, to name a few.
   - Stamp designs may even provide ideas for other art projects. For example, how about making a larger, but different, version of a modern design? Try changing shapes and colors. Or use colored

construction paper scraps to make Picasso-like designs. These projects may motivate children to take a peek at "the real picture" done by the artist in question.

5. *Catalogs* that feature pictures of toys and fashions, as well as articles from womens' magazines are good sources of teaching ideas.

6. *Cookie cutters* make fine decorative designs on paper and cardboard. If larger stencils are needed, try using pictures from *coloring books*. Mount them on cardboard, cut them out, and you have stencils that can be used immediately!

7. *Copper wire* makes fine jewelry, such as rings, pins, and bracelets. Encourage children to draw their designs on scrap paper before they attempt to bend wire in decorative shapes. Remind them that unwanted kinks in this wire will often spoil an excellent design. Other pupils may wish to try their hands in making wire animals and posing them in various settings and standing positions. (*Note:* A book entitled *Fun with Wire* by Joseph Leeming (J. B. Lippincott, 1956) is a good source for other wire ideas.) More complicated animals can be made by building up wire skeletons with papier-mâché newspaper strips.

8. *Coupons* that mother cannot use and/or labels from soup and other canned goods make fine reading and math materials. For various "match" activities, pupils may cut out individual letters or words. Don't forget recipes and weights of items given in English and metric measurements. Use coupons to compute how much money is actually saved by buying certain items. Or paste individual coupons on sheets of paper and write a problem right next to it.

9. *Crayons* should not be discarded because they happen to be too small to use comfortably. Besides rolling them on paper to achieve different effects, crayon pieces can be placed on a sunny windowsill and used for art projects when they soften.

10. *Curtain rings* can be used as counters, game pieces or parts of handmade jewelry.

11. *Decks of playing cards* used in adult and childrens' games should be saved, regardless of how many cards are missing from the deck. These cards can often be recycled into new card games or used in counting and other math activities.

12. *Discarded hats and clothing* make handy costumes for those class plays or role-playing. If an item is clean, but unfit for wear, see if pieces of fur or fabric can be salvaged first. For an unusual project, try making a large ventriloquist's dummy from childrens' discarded hats, jackets, shirts, pants and shoes.

13. *Discarded games* provide more game pieces, usable playing boards and ideas for new games. Place these parts in separate smaller boxes labeled for this purpose.

14. *Empty baby food jars* can double as extra paste pots—instantly! Simply wash them out and use them as needed. If you prefer using glue, empty Clairol hair dye bottles (the plastic squeeze type) can be rinsed out and filled with glue.

15. *Empty coffee, juice, and soup cans* should be cleaned and saved, if possible. Besides holding any variety of items such as pencils and rulers, these containers are handy for use in math and science activities.

16. *Envelopes* of every kind, including those from so-called "junk mail," should be saved. First remove unwanted address labels by pressing a 2-inch strip of cellophane tape on the label—and pulling both the tape and the label off. While all sizes of envelopes are useful, larger envelopes are particularly handy for use as impromptu puppets.

17. *Folders, pamphlets and other promotional literature* from various tourist offices and business firms have many recycling possibilities. Use them for making posters, booklets, murals and displays. Sometimes, figures of people and animals may be cut out, mounted on cardboard and used as puppets . . . or be cut apart to be included in background scenery.

18. *Foreign money* may be used in role-playing situations or as a source of inspiration for art and math activities.

19. *Gadgets* such as nuts, bolts and screws may be used for sorting and classifying purposes.

20. *Greeting cards* can be cut apart and used for classroom decorations, creative writing ideas and references for certain holiday details.

21. *Jar lids* make fine key chains. Before giving these lids to children to use, punch a hole at the top of each lid. Then have your pupils use colored paper and/or pictures to cut out and glue directly on the lids. Or, cut pieces of felt to size and glue them directly on the lid. At any rate, once a chain is threaded into the lid's hole, and keys are placed on this chain, this item will not easily be lost.

22. *Large buttons* make good eyes for puppets and dolls, game pieces for bingo, useful chips in trade games and markers in checkers.

23. *Local maps* may be used in studies of the community or state, as well as math problems involving times and travel locations.

24. *Magazines* are good sources for pictures, examples of words that begin with a certain letter, and ideas for creative writing and art projects.

25. *Milk containers* can be used for all kinds of art-construction projects, including unusual types of buildings, free-form constructions, mobiles, puppet heads, marionette bodies and bulletin board containers to hold those easily lost puzzle pieces, etc.

26. *Mirrors* can serve as ice for skating figurines, puppet shows and science projects.

27. *Newspapers* often contain useful weather maps, coupons, pictures, game ideas, interesting information and cartoons to motivate creative writing projects.

28. *Old paint brushes* often make useful instruments for cleaning out those hard-to-reach corners in equipment.

29. *Picture frames* may be used with cardboard cartons for

instant puppet theaters, as well as to emphasize certain bulletin board pictures and other features.

30. *Plastic bags* can be stapled to a large felt board to hold such art materials as clay or cloth scraps, wool and childrens' smaller unfinished projects.

31. *Plastic containers* make good beginnings for puppet heads *and* large figures. Using the container itself as a "body," attach a rubber (or tennis) ball to the top, and your figure is complete. Except, of course, for the clothes, which children can readily fashion from construction paper and bits of scrap fabrics. (See Figure 1-7.)

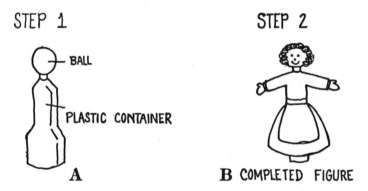

STEP 1

BALL

PLASTIC CONTAINER

A

STEP 2

B COMPLETED FIGURE

Figure 1-7

32. *Plastic shopping bags* can be used to hold wet hats and mittens.

33. *Pockets* (from discarded jeans) can be used to hold items such as pencils and small crafts projects— depending on how large the pockets are. These are especially handy if stapled in appropriate places on bulletin boards or learning centers.

34. *Postcards* are great for inspiring creative writing *and* as mini-jigsaw puzzles. Draw jigsaw puzzle shapes on picture side of the postcard. After placing and pasting the address side of the card face down on a corresponding piece of cardboard, cut out jigsaw shapes. The pieces can be placed in a small box and used.

35. *Price tags* of all kinds can be saved and used in a make-believe store by pupils.

36. *Roll-on deodorant sticks* make good markers. To use, remove the "ball" from the top of the container and refill the container with powder paint mixed with a small amount of water.

37. *Shampoo bottles,* especially the unbreakable kind, lend themselves as submarines for science experiments, foundations for bodies of dolls and figures, and used as simple jewelry pieces.

38. *Sponges* can be cut into any variety of letter and number shapes, bulletin board figures, and noiseless "blocks."

39. *Styrofoam* that is often found in packing, appears in a number of sizes, forms, and textures. Smaller bits of this stuff make fine ready-made "snow" for bulletin boards and may even suggest possibilities for dioramas and other crafts.

40. *Straps* from handbags also appear in a variety of fabrics, lengths and widths. Canvas straps are especially useful for recycling into book straps, bookmarks, etc. If wide enough, these straps may be tacked or taped nearby a bulletin board. Paper figures and childrens' worksheets can easily be pinned or stapled to these straps.

41. *String* of all colors and lengths serve many purposes. Use odd bits of string for miniature (cardboard) loom weaving, puppet hair, "string" pictures, string painting and macrame projects.

42. *Wooden telephone company reels,* when cleaned and painted, lend themselves to colorful classroom furniture or foundations for bulletin boards and other displays.

43. *Textured items* such as corrugated cardboard, velvet and other fabrics can be included in a "feely" box, or used for puppet costumes and features, diorama displays, lettering for bulletin boards and other items. (A "feely" box can be made from an empty shoe box. A slit wide enough to accommodate a child's hand is cut on

the cover. Then, textured items are placed within and the box is taped shut.)

44. *Tongue depressors* or ice cream sticks may be included in various craft projects as well as for math aids like rulers and counters.

45. *Traffic signs* may be copied on similarly shaped cardboard pieces and used in the classroom to teach bicycle safety.

46. *Wire ties* from bread and cake wrappers are well worth saving, for they often work better than string or thread in tying up smaller craft projects.

47. *Used train tickets* make useful patterns for trading cards or better yet, can be used as cards themselves.

48. *Wall paper sample books* contain durable paper for painting and fingerpainting projects. Use whole books to press leaves, flowers and pictures.

49. *Wood scraps,* when painted, make attractive blocks or stands (with a nail driven into the middle of each stand) for modelling puppet heads. Smaller pieces can be used to make pendants, bracelet "charms" and game markers.

50. *Wooden toothpicks and clay* make good materials for instant construction, such as models of buildings as well as geometrical math aids—squares, rectangles and triangles.

OTHER SOURCES YOU CAN PUT TO WORK

In this section, you will find some everyday items that are worth your efforts to obtain and recycle for your class' needs. Certain items may make interesting, novel teaching aids. Yet others are worth investigating further because they may give you just the ideas you've probably been seeking, but weren't sure where to look.

1. *Discarded election and campaign posters* have obvious possibilities in social studies units, but can also serve as reading aids and sources of "free" cardboard.

2. *Christmas ornaments,* or parts of them, may be recycled into more original creations.

3. *Cereal box offers* should be checked for possible games and/or learning aid ideas. Most of them are available for a nominal fee. If they seem suitable, they may be worth the small investment.

4. *Discarded dolls with movable parts,* when dressed of course, are fine as additions to still life scenes and as drawing models.

5. *Craft books,* even on the adult level, often suggest projects that can be adapted to meet the needs of your class.

6. *Current popular songs* are good idea sources, particularly for language arts activities. The so-called "protest songs" are worth exploring also.

7. *Local courses* that emphasize such areas as music, creative writing and art may offer new ideas you can try with children. Look into them anyway, and if you have the time or inclination, sign up!

8. *Adult puzzle—math diversions* need not be directly used with children, but their possibilities might. Games that involve strategy, for example, may be adapted to help reinforce thinking skills.

2

ACTIVITIES TO HELP PUPILS THINK CREATIVELY

Projects such as painting, puppetry or poetry offer various ways for children to experiment with colors, shapes and words. In painting a mural, for example, children must decide what figures to include, if any, and a color scheme. With puppets, there is plenty of room for trial-and-error as far as characters are concerned. Poetry, too, offers children opportunities to play with thoughts via words. However, with poetry you can also encourage your pupils to think creatively for the sheer fun of it—and help reinforce their reading skills at the same time. (Or, to make constructive use of "free" time.)

Try, for example, working with the situations under the "Just Suppose" heading as one way of stimulating pupils' imaginations. Children can also dramatize their ideas in role playing.

SITUATIONS THAT CALL FOR QUICK THINKING

Just Suppose. Pupils take turns in giving the most ridiculous situation and challenging each other to devise ingenious solutions for getting out of it, such as:

- A certain time machine is only good for going back in time. As you leave it, you find that you left your valuable watch inside. What do you do to get it back?
- While watching TV, you find that they have announced almost all of the numbers of a lottery ticket you own. Just as the announcer is getting ready to say the last (winning?) number, the TV goes blank. Everything you do to

get the TV back in working order doesn't seem to help. Your friend lives too far away and neither of you have telephones. What do you do? (Buying a paper the next day won't help; you also happen to owe some money, and must know immediately if you've won or not.)

- You suddenly win $100,000. Some of your friends want to ask you for a loan. What do you do or say to them?

- A friend is being chased by someone, and as he's running, he hands you a bag of valuables and yells out for you to safeguard them. In about five minutes, think of as many different good hiding places as you can.

- At a party, you are suddenly called upon to make a speech about an important guest of honor. You had no time to prepare it. What do you do and what do you say?

- Make up your own situation:

    You have a _____ but _____, etc.

TELLING TALL TALES AND THEN SOME

1. *Pull a Tale.* You will need a set of 3 × 5-inch cards. On each card, paste part of a magazine picture or print a word. Each player draws two cards and tries to tell an impromptu tale: the wilder, the better.

2. *Classroom Mystery Letter.* Write a letter to the class—or have a pupil write one—containing the middle part or end of a ridiculous story. Pupils may tell the rest of the story orally or in writing.

3. *Toy Figure Tales.* Place a few toy figures on a small table in front of a card with the following directions: "What is going on over here?" "Make up a story telling what you think will happen and how things will end."

4. *I Heard It Over the Radio.* Choose one pupil to make up an imaginary radio announcement and tell in one sentence. Give other children a chance to add to the story. If the story reaches an ideal ending before all of the students have had a chance to contribute, another story can be started, beginning with those pupils who didn't get a turn.

5. *Top This.* Have pupils pretend to own the largest cake,

the biggest boat, etc., and challenge their partner to come up with something even better.

6. *How I Solved It.* Have pupils make up a complicated problem, or supply them with one. Ask for solutions to fit one or more of the following categories: the shortest, the funniest, the most clever, the most impossible, the most logical, the saddest, the most complicated, the least complicated.

7. *Tall Tale in a Word.* Find all of the possible smaller words in a longer word such as "overbearing." Take all of these smaller words and use them in a story.

8. *Story Volleyball.* Divide the class into two groups and assign a leader to each one. Groups then take turns in completing the beginning of a story by one of the other groups. The groups that are able to continue the story without stopping win.

9. *Simulation Story.* Have two pupils dramatize a short street or school scene for the class, and have the audience pretend to be reporters. After the dramatization, ask the class reporters to write the story they'd report to tomorrow's newspaper. Aim for a newspaper-style story.

10. *Funny Stories.* Use favorite jokes to develop funny stories.

USING OBJECTS TO INSPIRE CREATIVITY

Next to words, objects such as small toys and pictures provide interesting starting points. They can help focus children's attention on various possibilities by answering such questions as:

"What other uses does this toy or gadget have?"

"If I turn it, changing its shape, what other thing or things will it look like?"

"How would I describe this thing—exactly—to someone who may not have seen or heard about it before?"

"What words would I use to describe this item if I were in a hurry? If I had a lot of time?"

"What does the name of the object mean, and can this meaning be put to further use?"

"Who might be able to make good use of this item now,
and why?"

"How else could this object be made? Could I make one
like it, only smaller or larger?"

Before answering any of those questions, children should be
able to examine the toy or picture closely. What size, color, or
shape is it? Does it feel smooth or hard? Furry or rough? Of
course, pupils will learn more about an item as they turn it over in
their hands and look at it. They will find out whether it makes a
loud noise if it accidentally falls on their desks. Perhaps children
remember another toy or picture exactly like it.

During this activity, try dividing the class in smaller groups,
and tell pupils to close their eyes as you have them take turns
handling a different object. Can they tell what they are touching
with their eyes closed? Ask pupils to describe their experiences or
draw impressions of what they thought they were handling.

Possible Objects

The following group of objects is only a partial list of items
that can be successfully explored by children. Feel free to pick and
choose, or better yet, find and work with your own interesting
combinations.

scissors	wooden cubes
coat hangers	ash trays
pie plates	paper clips
empty juice cans	pom poms
large beads	paperweights
spools	doorknobs
different lengths of string	rulers
ribbon or wool	construction paper shapes
dice	corks
stuffed toy animals	yo-yos
fingers from gloves	crumpled colored cellophane
mirrors	various picture postcards
broken clocks	discarded bicycle wheels

A Few Examples to Help Your Class Be Creative

Scissors. Use the size and shape of scissors as aids to drawing or modelling imaginary inventions, people and animal patterns. Trace parts of scissors against pieces of scenery for certain surreal effects. This scenery may include pictures from magazines or newspapers, or even scenes drawn by the children themselves. Ideally, these scenes should only include items such as mountains, buildings and trees. They should be free of smaller details that would tend to clutter the overall design. What other uses can scissors have?

Spools. What can be done with two halves of a spool? With one half? How could its shape be changed so it will still look like a spool? What else could be wrapped around a giant spool? Can there be such a thing as a shrinking/stretching spool? If so, what would it look like? What could the hole at the spool's center contain? Could people get along without spools for long? Suppose all of the spools disappeared, what would happen? Tell a story, Kipling-style, of the first spool and how it came to be. Make up sayings ending in ". . . like a spool."

Mirrors. What other stories include the use of mirrors besides the fairy tale "Snow White and the Seven Dwarfs." Suppose you looked in a mirror and found that your reflection was slowly disappearing: what would you think? Make up your own superstition about mirrors and build up a myth around it. What would you do with a giant mirror? Your own funhouse mirror? Try to imagine a very soft, melting mirror, using Dali's paintings as an example. Build up a story around these possibilities. Suppose you never saw a mirror before: how would you react? What would be the first thing you did? Use a mirror to make a picture of a maze in reverse, then try solving that maze. Also, design a greeting card, using a mirror as part of the design.

Doorknobs. What other things could doorknobs be made to do? What kind of doorknob was featured in the story "Alice in Wonderland"? What other materials could doorknobs be made of? Suppose you tried to turn a doorknob and couldn't: does this always mean that the door is locked? What else could it mean? Suppose you squeezed a doorknob and made it get smaller each time? How could this have happened? What other names can you think of besides the word "doorknob"? Name ten other substitutes for a doorknob. Describe an unusual doorknob so well that everyone knows exactly what kind you mean. How would aliens from outer space use a doorknob if they thought of other uses for it? What are some of the things you could make from a doorknob?

Discarded bicycle wheels. How many ways can a bicycle wheel be turned so that it no longer looks like a bicycle wheel? Try to imagine a different kind of motorcycle which has wheels that are bicycle wheels. What would it look like? Draw a picture of it or make a model of it. What else could be done with these shapes? Would a wider bicycle wheel have more advantages?

PUTTING CREATIVITY BACK INTO CREATIVE WRITING

When a child is turned on by an idea and uses it to write creatively, you can be sure that he made that idea his own in some way. Perhaps his own background and feelings were easily related to that idea. Perhaps one idea led to another and another, allowing the child to choose among many possibilities. Finally, one choice was preferred over all of the rest, and in the end, that child had enough material for the beginnings of a possible story or poem.

What has this got to do with improving creative writing? Plenty! Often, throwing various ideas at children is not enough. For, to use these ideas effectively, children must be able to draw from their own backgrounds, experiences, and most of all, they must be able to care. Then finding something to write about doesn't seem so overwhelming. And all of those ideas and devices provide enough material for pupils to think about. Below are some starters that can help children get a head start on creative writing:

1. *Block of "Happenings."* Paste magazine pictures or words on each side of a large cardboard block. To use, toss once to get the beginning or an idea of a story, then toss again to find out what other "happening" can be linked with the first. (See Figure 2-1.)

2. *"You are There" Journal.* Journal writing is often suggested as one way of motivating children to write creatively. While you can have children begin by writing about their own experiences, you will both be pleased with the results from a different viewpoint. Have chil-

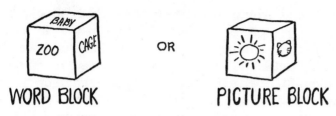

Figure 2-1

dren pretend that a friend, parent or other person is writing them a letter. What do they think about a holiday? Does it bring back memories of a childhood spent at the shore, the mountains, or even in a foreign land? What else would this ongoing letter say? Or choose someone completely different. For example, what would a particular comic book hero/heroine/character write in such a journal? How would he or she feel if he or she was the last person on earth—after everyone has moved to another planet?

USING EVERYDAY EXPERIENCES TO GET IDEAS

Before asking children to write, have them spend some time in a "brainstorming" session. You may choose to work with the class as a whole, or with smaller groups of pupils.

The easiest way to begin is by asking pupils to name experiences they may have had, such as going to a party or playing ball in the neighborhood lot. List each experience on the board or on a large piece of wrapping paper.

Next to this section, make another list. You may want to give this list a name such as "Scenes" or "Settings." Under this heading, list places children may have heard of, seen, or studied about. Almost any place would be acceptable. Examples may include "a garden," "the moon," "a used-car lot," "an island," and so on.

Finally, ask volunteers in your class to name a few possible events. A good name for this list might be happenings and examples of such happenings may include a mysterious map (or letter) is found," "someone is chasing a thief when all of a sudden . . .," "a newcomer to town loses his way, and . . ." Using similar examples, children have a chance to answer the questions who, what, why, and where in their stories—which should be kept vague for this reason. If possible, children may wish to expand these lists to include other categories like "People" (a cowboy, a school child, detective, cook, truck driver, etc.), "Time" (last week, last month, the year 3000, a music beat, etc.), or "Animals" (bear, cat, dog, alligator, or tiger).

The next step, of course, is to invite your pupils "to make something of it." For openers, have them choose a place and happening from the lists on the board. Pose questions like "What happened next?" "And then what?" Sometimes drawing a picture helps a few children to visualize a scene and write about it. Much depends on the age of your pupils and how comfortable they feel with a scene or happening. Whenever possible, ask children to begin with an item they feel most comfortable with, for they will be able to invent other happenings and details. During this time, encourage children to do as much as they can with these stories.

At some later date, you may assign pupils in smaller groups, giving them the opportunity to share their stories with classmates and get instant feedback. This is also a good time to assist individual children who need further direction. Also, correcting stories can be made into a learning experience for older pupils. Try explaining what a few frequently used proofreading symbols mean and have children correct their stories using these marks.

In the end, use pupils' final versions of stories as further motivation. One ambitious, worthwhile activity involves mimeographing favorite stories of the class and including them in a class magazine. Perhaps interested class members can contribute their drawing and organizing talents.

To encourage children to practice their writing skills, write each happening, scene and experience on separate 3 × 5-inch cards, or ask pupils to help do this. After obtaining and decorating three shoe boxes with paint or wrapping paper, attach one label to each box. Then place each group of cards in its respective box. A caption such as "Reach for a Story" or "Make-a-Story Center" should be made and placed near these boxes.

More Story Starters

1. *Pantomime first—then set the scene by role playing.* Before the actual writing begins, ask for a volunteer or

two, or pantomime a series of actions and have the class guess what is happening, and then use their imagination to tell what might happen next. The following list includes a few open examples children can try, either individually or in a group of two or three: (Children will have to make up their own answers to the questions What? Why? When? Who? and How?):

Lift something heavy. (What? Why? Who?)

Walk, but keep looking back. (Who is following you?)

Stop a passerby on the street. (What kind of information will you ask him or her for? What should he or she be aware of?—An open pot hole, a slippery area, etc.)

Pick up something from the sidewalk. (What did you find? Money? A note? What was in the note? Was anyone watching?)

Look around, anxiously. (Who or what are you afraid of? Why?)

Wave at someone. (Who? From where and why?)

Exercise in front of a mirror, and see _____.

Tug at something. (What? Why? Who?)

Answer a phone. (Who? What? When? Where?)

Look for something. (What? Why?)

Ignore someone. (Where? Why? How?)

Scare someone. (Where? Why? Who?)

Open something. (What? Why? Who? Where?)

Hide something. (What? Why? Who? Where?)

Then let the children use their imaginations to describe on paper what they think is happening and what happens next. The sentences describing what happens next need not be very many at first; two or three sentences will be fine. Allow a few minutes for children to do this. When they all are done, call on volunteers to role play the situation from the beginning, but only for a few minutes. By now, most children may have ideas of their own!

2. *Those Were the Days.* Relive an important day of your life and then write a story about it. This time, think of

how that day might have been different if _____
did or did not happen.

3. *Cartoon Stories.* Cut out a cartoon from the paper.
   Then write a story around it, filling in the beginning,
   middle or ending.

4. *What Does Your Deejay Say?* Did you really listen to the
   radio this morning? Did you hear the announcer's or
   deejay's jokes? If you remember them, you just might
   have the beginning of a story. On the other hand, you
   may want to try your hand at making up some deejay
   chatter, and getting ideas from that. Is there any way to
   change and/or exaggerate a deejay's stories?

5. *That's Nothing!* Or try to exaggerate a story or event as
   much as possible, without letting it get out of hand. To
   help get ideas started, ask the question "What if?" Then
   answer it with the wildest exaggeration you can think
   of.

6. *Title Story.* Make up various story titles around a word.
   List a few likely words to build a title around and work
   with those first, such as:

   Happy
   Missing
   Broken
   Storm
   Cat
   Mystery of _____

7. *Scrambled Story.* Paste one picture each on separate
   pieces of blank paper. Add more pages if you like. Then
   rearrange these pages and use them to make up a story.
   For a new story, mix these pages up again and place
   them in a different order.

8. *He Said, She Said.* Listen to an actual conversation or
   get someone's quote from the newspaper. Then try to
   determine what led to that person's remark and what
   happened next. Or build a story around a wise saying,
   such as "Haste makes waste."

9. *In Other Words.* You will need a dictionary or thesaurus

to find a long word such as "extraordinary." Using the letters in this word, beginning with the first letter, find other smaller words. Finally try using all of these smaller words in a story—including the original big word.

10. *Word Clues.* Find and cut out individual words from old magazines and newspapers. Place all of these words in a hat, box or bag, mix them up and randomly draw three or four words. Using these words, can you make up a story that sounds logical, and yet interesting?

3

MAKING THE MOST OF "CLASSROOM COMMUNICATORS"

As you know, good bulletin boards are well worth the time and effort spent on them. They are often sources of worthwhile learning experiences, for they offer plenty to do or think about. In addition, these boards are sources of new ideas for you, and they need not always be time-consuming.

For example, if you're really pressed for time, you will be glad to know of various ways to work with a subject you may have in mind, or help to extend a unit your class happens to be working on.

On the other hand, if you have spare time, why not invest it in generating original ideas? To do this, consider the ideas which are included for building around a theme. Usually, you will be able to think of more ideas than you can record in a single attempt.

EASY WAYS TO BUILD AROUND A THEME

As you use themes, you will find that school subjects may offer just the material you need—other than facts children must study and so on. For a change, try making use of another aspect of a science or social studies unit. You can enhance your class's study of the Middle Ages, for example, with a short-notice bulletin board about King Arthur's Court, or with ballads made up by wandering minstrels. This could lead to individual activities involving longer poems and even songs about living in the city, seeing a lost pet again, traveling to another city or state, and so on.

Many times, magazine articles provide other sources of inspiration and ideas you can use to meet the needs of your class. Try such articles for helpful information about current events, holidays, well-known personalities, music, art and foreign lands.

In a magazine article about energy, for example, you may find enough material for the beginnings of a fine bulletin board. This board can be simple, focusing on energy conservation or it can be somewhat more elaborate, focusing on the sources of energy and their various uses. Bring in the related math, science and social studies that your class is currently working on. By all means include language arts in the way of "energy" word puzzles, stories and skits. Ask children to imagine what would happen if we had to get along without energy for just one day. If you include these and artwork possibilities on separate activity cards, you will have indeed provided a variety of worthwhile learning experiences. Other sources of themes include the following:

- *Sports* (in appropriate seasons) such as baseball, basketball, ice-skating, football and tennis.

  Possible Activities and Beginnings: Find and use legends and/or poems about a sport, for example, "Casey at the Bat" (language arts and social studies); practice giving and following directions in the order given (language arts); make up cheers (language arts); find out how a given sport began, as well as something about that period of history (social studies and language arts); compute, compare and graph statistical information shown in team records (math); heroes and heroines and how they became interested in pursuing a particular calling, adventure or sport (language arts, social studies); writing a "pretend" journal as a great sports personality might have written it (language arts); a _____ sports Hall of Fame (language arts, art, social studies); preparation needed to excel at a sport (health, science).

- *Probability*, or "Laws or Chance" can lead to further consideration of Pascal's Triangle (math); experiments with probability (math); finding out if luck is involved and exploring related superstitions (social studies and language arts); probability of a team favorite or underdog winning or losing.

- *Number Puzzles.* Make a collection of puzzles for a class book (language arts); finding as many solutions as possible for a given puzzle (math); doing simple computations in addition and multiplication as the ancient Egyptians did (math and social studies); figuring out strategies in chess and/or *Monopoly* (language arts, math); finding out what certain numbers meant to ancient peoples (social studies); finding out the origins of chess (social studies), and so on.

If you have a few spare minutes, put them to good use by generating more themes. Here's how: deliberately choose a broad area, like science, and finally narrow it down to "studies about the ocean," and grab a pencil and scrap paper.

Keeping your grade level in mind, you might further narrow this subject to "seashore" and write down every word that is even vaguely related to the sea. Try to avoid rejecting any word off-hand. The time to stop is when you can no longer think of any likely words. In the end, your list will provide you with a good range of possible topics, regardless of its length. Your results may look something like this:

Ocean—seashore, shells, fish, summer, vacation, underwater life, sharks, *Jaws*, clams, seafood, sand, Moby Dick, whales, boating, sailors, sea ditties, sea stories, mermaids, tuna, anchors, divers, pearls, buried treasure, pirates, schooners, explorers, maps, Atlantis, ancient Greek and Roman "sea myths," ancient sailors, Phoenicians, Minoans, etc.

As you glance over your list, feel free to cross out irrelevant words or phrases whose possibilities seem too limited or advanced. But don't eliminate them completely. Later on, you may find that such words are further sources of ideas.

By now, you should try to imagine each remaining word on your list as a starting point of a bulletin board idea about the sea. Perhaps a word seems to suggest one or more related words. Write them down! If you can practically "see" a good background scene, take a few seconds to work with it a bit more and make a rough sketch of it. Then get ready to explore its possibilities. You can do this by relating the idea or topic to other areas of the curriculum. Is there any way you can extend classwork in social studies, language arts, music or art? Is there any information to draw from in children's nonfiction and fiction books? (These books should be investigated first, if possible. Their pictures and topics are excellent sources of ideas you can use to build on.)

If you group words such as "sea myths," "divers" and "Minoans" together, you will most likely get interesting results for a science fiction story. Just for fun, add other related words to this list. Now choose any two or three of them, and see if you can add to what you already have. Experiment a bit more. This time, try omitting one of those words and substituting others. Even if you decide on a related theme or one that's entirely different, remember that you will have obtained a few new ideas as well.

Good ideas appear in many sources. In looking for words in respective categories, look in your thesaurus, children's books, and songs, too. In the meantime, save cartoons, pictures, jokes and other materials. They are sources of ideas as well!

BULLETIN BOARD MATERIALS—FOR LETTERS, BACKGROUND AND FIGURES

After deciding what figures and activities to include with your particular theme, you can easily take care of more practical matters, beginning with letters.

Letters

Since a bulletin board's attractiveness and usefulness is enhanced by good lettering, it seems worthwhile to spend more time in making them. You know, for example, that new sets of letters or words must be carefully measured and cut out for each new bulletin board. You may also find yourself constantly replacing old letters with new ones. If these letters will be about the same size for succeeding bulletin boards, you can save time by tracing around them (to make letters of other colors) as well as by making your own stencils in one of two ways.

First, salvage those "old" letters further by gluing them to cardboard and cutting them out after allowing enough drying time. Place them in a specially marked box.

The second way takes somewhat longer, but will save you much time with subsequent bulletin boards. Begin by drawing the necessary letters on sheets of drawing paper, and gluing each sheet to separate pieces of cardboard. Allow enough drying time. Later, carefully cut out each letter and your stencils are completed. To make them more durable, use shellac or cellophane tape. Try placing tape on the surfaces, not the edges of each letter.

Still another way to make larger stencils is by drawing a letter on 8½ × 11-inch cardboard (see Fig. 3-1A) and carefully cutting it out. If you cut the letter in the middle, as shown in Figure 3-1B, you will have made two stencils (as shown in Figures 3-1C and 3-1D).

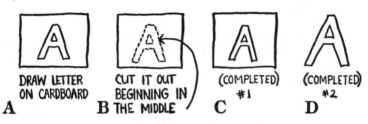

DRAW LETTER ON CARDBOARD **A**   CUT IT OUT BEGINNING IN **B** THE MIDDLE   (COMPLETED) #1 **C**   (COMPLETED) #2 **D**

Figure 3-1

If you would like to try three-dimensional letters for a change, gather the following materials: newspaper, scissors, adhesive tape and paint. First, roll the newspaper sheets, cut to desired length, tape and bind them in the appropriate letter-shape, hold in place with adhesive tape, and paint as shown in Figure 3-2.

ROLL NEWSPAPER SHEET **A**   CUT TO DESIRED LENGTH AND TAPE **B** THE ROLL IN PLACE   BEND THIS ROLL TO APPROPRIATE **C** SHAPE AND PAINT

Figure 3-2

For making letters quickly and easily, there's nothing quite like magic markers. Using their bright colors enables you to highlight activity cards and envelopes. If you like, you can define the brighter colors with a contrasting darker color, and complete the bulletin board caption in less time than you would expect.

For more textured effects, try using rope, ribbon or braiding to form words in cursive writing. By doing this, you will be able to "connect" the succeeding letters of a word without having to come to a complete stop after each letter in the words you have chosen. First measure the desired size of these words and write the caption carefully in pencil on the bulletin board itself. Then cover this outline with one strand of rope or braiding, holding it in place at intervals with cellophane tape.

Background

For most short-notice bulletin boards, simply tape the caption and figures directly to the bulletin board surface. In some cases, a background as such is unnecessary—the neutral color of the class bulletin board or blackboard often works well enough.

Try to imagine your bulletin board with and without a background. Does it seem more attractive without one or not? To avoid covering everything, you should consider a partial background. And here's where a large geometrical shape or two consisting of construction paper sheets or strips can be used to the best advantage as seen in Figure 3-3.

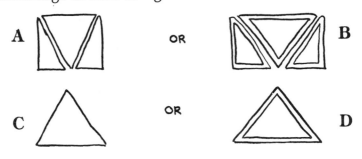

Figure 3-3

Bulletin Board Figures

These can be made of a variety of the following materials—large magazine pictures, movie posters and coloring books, as well as cardboard figures of people, animals and items from previous bulletin boards.

WHAT DOES TIME MEAN TO YOU?

To add a little magic to those lessons about time, try drawing on the language arts as well as social studies and math. This will extend children's learning experiences in a fascinating topic at the same time. The short-notice bulletin board in Figure 3-4 shows only one of many possibilities. It may even give you ideas for other bulletin boards and activities! To make it, draw, trace, or cut out figures of animals from coloring or picture books. On large sheets of wrapping paper, use felt-tipped magic markers for writing questions and captions. If you have more time, try forming

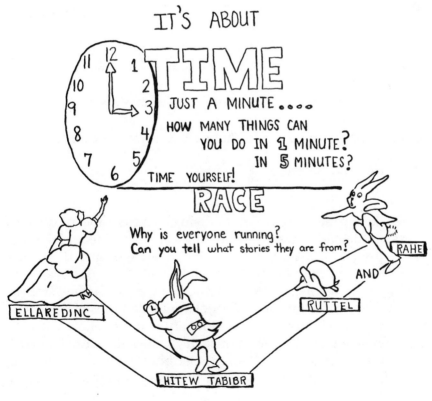

Figure 3-4

caption words from construction paper, fabric or felt. You may also want to include large envelopes to hold activity sheets and pupils' work.

You can also enhance your class's study of time and the calendar by making and using a model of an ancient calendar. A version of the one used by the Romans is pictured in the children's book, *Time in Your Life* by Irving Adler (John Day Co., New York) or *Clocks, Calendars and Carousels* by John Gabriel Navarra, (Doubleday & Co., New York). During this time, some pupils in your class may be interested in discovering what the first calendars looked like, why the signs of the zodiac were included, and about the myths connected with the names of days and months. It will certainly be well worth your time to encourage pupils by providing any or all of the books listed below:

Adler, Irving, *Time in Your Life*, The John Day Co., New York.

Bell, Thelma Harrington, *The Riddle of Time*, The Viking Press, New York.

Bradley, Duane, *Time for You*, J. B. Lippincott Co., Philadelphia, Pa.

Navarra, John Gabriel, *Clocks, Calendars, and Carousels*, Doubleday & Co., New York.

Neal, Harry Edward, *The Mystery of Time*, Julian Messner, New York, 1966.

Zarchy, Harry, *Wheel of Time*, Thomas Y. Crowell, New York.

Other Related Activities

Math/Science

Make up and do problems using various time records in sports, particularly where the Olympics are concerned. Make and use a sundial. What are some of its advantages and disadvantages? Find out how the water clock and the hourglass worked. Making a model of a water clock might be a worthwhile science project. For further information, look for illustrations of these and other clocks in childrens' books. Identify and learn how the constellations were used. Models of such constellations can be made using oatmeal boxes. See children's astronomy books for pictures and directions. Find out what part the seasons played in ancient people's lives.

Social Studies/Language Arts

Find out about some of the more famous clocks, such as Big Ben. What are other ways people used to tell time? How did sailors tell time long ago? What are some of the legends behind the signs of the zodiac? What is astrology? Why did the ancient Babylonians believe in it? Make a collection of "time" expressions, such as "Time flies," "Time waits for no one," "Time is money," "The early bird gets the worm," "Time will tell" and "Good timing!"

Art

Illustrate and dramatize some "time myths." Use zodiac signs as further inspiration for jewelry and other crafts projects. What did some of the older clocks look like? Using cardboard cartons, make replicas of them.

PUT THESE STATES IN THEIR PLACES!

A few weeks before vacation time, try using a different topic such as "Travel—U.S.A." to motivate your pupils and reinforce their language and map-reading skills, or to enrich those geography lessons and units. With this bulletin board, for example, your class will quickly discover that there is indeed something in it for everyone.

Moreover, the materials for this board are easy to make or obtain. The "center of attraction," of course, is a large map of the United States which you may obtain ready-made and usually free—or you can make one yourself. In this case, simply use an opaque projector to enlarge the map and trace a copy of it on a large piece of wrapping paper. Again, you may find that using magic markers for lettering is convenient and makes for attractive results as well. You will also need three large envelopes for such features as "Missing Capitals," "Licenses" and "State Folders." Here is where those used business and junk mail envelopes can be put to good use. Finally, a shoe box or a similar carton may hold slips of paper with names of states. Or you can have a pupil draw and cut out individual "state shapes" using colored construction paper. As pupils complete various projects, such as folders, you may wish to add them on to another "travel display." (See Figure 3-5.)

Other Related Activities

Math

Find out which states are included under certain time zones, such as "Mountain Time." Compare the sizes of individual state cardboard pieces; measure them, using English and metric systems. Choose a small area of your own state and find as many shortcuts to and from another given city as possible. Where do some of the main highways and train routes lead?

Social Studies

Make posters designed to attract tourists to the state or states of your choice. Look at other kinds of maps of the United States: weather, topological maps, etc. What do their legends mean? Pick out a place you would like to visit and choose a scenic route to take in getting there—or, make up your own such route. Pretend that you will have a visitor with you. Find out what states well-known people from different fields were born in. Take a survey. Learn to read a road map. Collect maps of different states by writing to state tourist offices. What places would you like to visit? How would you get there? What attractions would you wish to visit first? Make up a different kind of state fair, featuring for example, only class paintings and similar crafts for your own state.

Language Arts

Make up a poem or ballad for your own state or one you would like to visit. Include in your state folder everything you'd like a tourist to see first. Make up a dictionary listing noteworthy features of the state. For example, "Alabama, A to Z."

Art

Make up a collage of various state shapes: first draw, then cut out state shapes from cardboard and arrange the individual pieces under a sheet of paper, coloring over it with a crayon.

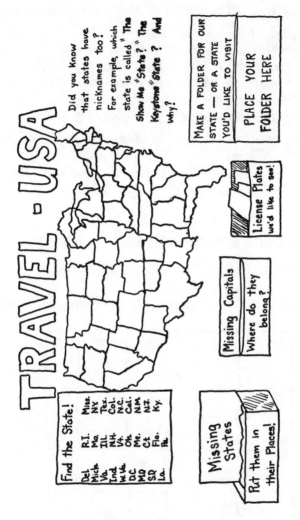

TRAVEL - USA

Did you know that states have nicknames too?

For example, which state is called "The Show Me 'State?' " The Keystone "State"? And why?

MAKE A FOLDER FOR OUR STATE — OR A STATE YOU'D LIKE TO VISIT

PLACE YOUR FOLDER HERE

License Plates we'd like to see!

Missing Capitals

Where do they belong?

Find the State!

Del.	R.I.	Miss.
Mich.	Ma.	N.Y.
Va.	Ill.	Tex.
Ind.	N.H.	Col.
W.Va.	Vt.	N.C.
D.C.	Oh.	Cal.
Md.	Me.	N.M.
S.D.	Ct.	N.J.
La.	Fla.	Ky.

Missing States

Put them in their Places!

Figure 3-5

57

Make a key chain of a state shape—using cardboard, wood or felt. Make up a large poster of your own state, including main cities and other places of interest. Make up a mobile (drawn on cardboard, of course) of your state's attractions. For further information, you may wish to consult any or all of the following:

Carpenter, Allan, *The New Enchantment of America: Pennsylvania,* Children's Press, Chicago, 1978. (Other books by the same author include those about Mississippi, Arkansas, Michigan, Maine, Louisiana, Alabama, Minnesota, Missouri, California, Colorado, South Dakota, New Mexico and Massachusetts.)

Edey, Maitland, *The Northeast Coast,* Time-Life Books, New York.

Malone, John, *An Album of the American Cowboy,* Franklin Watts, New York, 1971.

Nolan, Jeannette, *Indiana,* Coward-McCann, New York, 1969.

Ross, George, *Know Your U.S.A.,* Rand McNally, & Co., New York, 1974.

WHAT'S MISSING HERE—AND WHY?

Many times, fun and challenge can provide a welcome change of pace while working to the pupils' best advantage. In this bulletin board, for example, there are pictures containing

Figure 3-6

missing or otherwise incomplete items. Pupils are challenged to find as many of these items as possible. As they enjoy playing detective, the children are also improving their observation and related language skills, for there are items to be found, named and described. The scenes in these line drawings are taken from such familiar settings as a birthday party, railroad station and the park. Such scenes may even remind some children of their own experiences in these settings and motivate others to talk or write about them. (See Figures 3-6 and 3-7.)

Best of all, you will find that of all bulletin boards, this one is probably the easiest and quickest to make. First cut a large silhouette of the detective peering through his magnifying glass

Figure 3-7

from black, purple or other dark-colored paper. Or you may prefer to use a large piece of wrapping paper to draw and cut out the detective's outline, and paint it a dark color afterwards. Or you can opt for drawing and coloring in his features before placing him on the bulletin board. For lettering, use magic markers, dark crayons, or cut letters from paper or cloth. Finally, place each picture in its appropriate place on the bulletin board. For variety, try changing pictures as soon as most of the children have had the opportunity to discover the missing items. One easy way of obtaining different pictures is by tracing suitable coloring book pages. Be sure to leave out some details before placing these pictures on display.

Figure 3-7 (continued)

Other Related Activities

Read about the adventures of storybook detectives such as Sherlock Holmes, Nancy Drew, and Inspector Clouseau (from the *Pink Panther*). Find out what detectives really do and use this information to make a career book about detectives and related police careers. To solve problems, detectives must often work with only a few clues. How do you use clues to solve such problems as finding a misplaced toy or book or even in playing

Figure 3-7 (continued)

"Hide-and-Seek"? Is it always easy to try to remember when, what, and how?

Find pictures of old time "Wanted" posters. Make up one of your own, using a real or make-believe person and ask your classmates to guess who that person is. Try making up a series of adventures for a detective you've made up; ask classmates to look at pictures you have drawn illustrating your story and tell what *they* think is happening.

Why were things like magnifying glasses used as "symbols" for detectives? Why are bloodhounds often used?

Make up your own versions of such favorite games as "Twenty Questions" and "Hangman."

Include pupils' answers as part of a separate bulletin board display entitled, "Found!"

ALL ABOUT DINOSAURS

Of all unusual creatures of the past, dinosaurs seem to be the most fascinating to children. And no wonder! For what child can resist knowing more about the large, often huge, sizes and strange shapes of dinosaurs? Or can resist trying to imagine these monsters living and roaming about on the earth? For these and similar reasons, a short-notice bulletin board about dinosaurs may prove to be a very popular classroom activity.

Although you can explore this topic from almost any angle, it is usually a good idea to begin with a board about dinosaurs in general, as in the example shown in Figure 3-8. Extend areas that seem to interest your class the most.

To make this bulletin board, obtain pictures of dinosaurs from books, pamphlets, or draw them yourself. In the following pages, you will see pictures of some familiar dinosaurs. Place each cut-out on the background as shown. Using colored construction paper, oaktag, or pieces of wrapping paper, cut out various shapes for activity sheets and write directions with magic markers. You will also need one or two large envelopes to hold smaller sets of activities. Display all of these features as shown in Figure 3-8 and your bulletin board is ready to use.

If possible, try including any or all of the following books for children's reference. Some of your pupils may be able to borrow these books from the library:

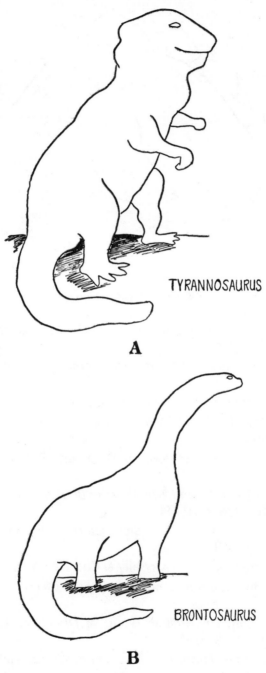

TYRANNOSAURUS

A

BRONTOSAURUS

B

Figure 3-8

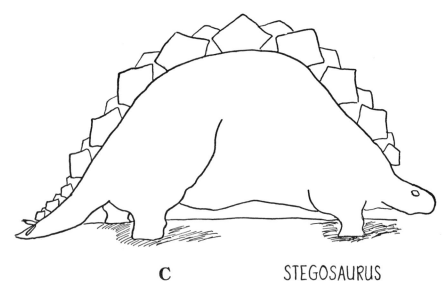

C   STEGOSAURUS

Figure 3-8 (continued)

Cohen, Daniel, *What Really Happened to the Dinosaurs?* E.P. Dutton, New York, 1977.

Colbert, Edwin, *Millions of Years Ago*, Thomas Y. Crowell, New York, 1958.

————, *The Dinosaur Book*, McGraw Hill, New York, 1951.

Craig, Jean, *Dinosaurs and More Dinosaurs*, Four Winds Press, New York, 1968.

Dickinson, Alice. *The First Book of Dinosaurs*, Franklin Watts, New York, 1964.

Geis, Darlene, *The How and Why Wonder Book of Dinosaurs*, Grosset & Dunlap, New York, 1960.

Ipsen, D.C., *The Riddle of the Stegosaurus*, Addison-Wesley, Massachusetts, 1969.

Know Your Dinosaurs, Rand McNally & Co., New York, 1977.

McGowan, Tom, *Album of Dinosaurs*, Rand McNally & Co., Chicago, 1972.

Ostrom, Dr. John, *The Strange World of Dinosaurs*, G.P. Putnam's Sons, New York, 1964.

Pringle, Lawrence. *Dinosaurs and Their World*, Harcourt Brace Jovanovich, New York, 1968.

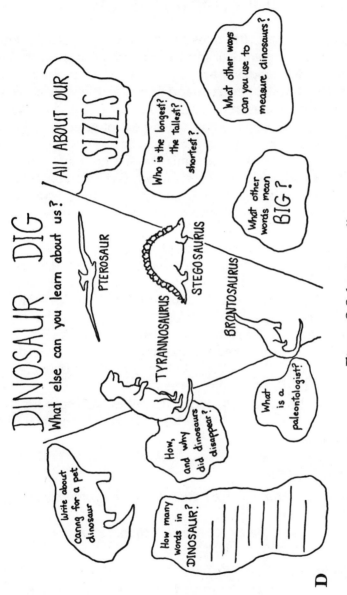

Figure 3-8 (continued)

EVERYTHING YOU ALWAYS WANTED TO KNOW ABOUT SCIENCE FICTION

In science fiction, the question "What if . . ." has been answered in many unheard-of (and often surprising) ways. There are monsters like Godzilla and Frankenstein's creation, heroes like Flash Gordon, Superman, and Wonder Woman, as well as intergalactic adventures in programs like *Star Trek* and movies like *Star Wars*. All of these elements are a part of science fiction and great fun. Best of all, they can often be used as sources to extend other learning experiences for your class. Certainly, science fiction reading can and should be included. But it can be the beginning of related building, thinking, and imagining activities. To start things off, choose a science fiction setting in outer space as shown in the example in Figure 3-9.

Use colored paper, oaktag, or cardboard to draw and cut out similar figures. For a contrasting color scheme, try dark blue or violet with scraps of tinfoil or yellow construction paper. After cutting out all the figures, use crayons or magic markers for lettering. Place these figures in appropriate places on the bulletin board. Later on, you may wish to take advantage of related activities as well as provide additional materials and books nearby. You will also find that science fiction offers children plenty of opportunities to display their work.

Although the following books are rather advanced for use by children, they offer much in the way of background material in science fiction.

A Few Helpful Books

Bretnor, Reginald (Ed.), *Science Fiction Today and Tomorrow*, Harper & Row, New York, 1974.

Brosman, John, *The Cinema of Science Fiction: Future Tense*, St. Martin's Press, New York, 1978.

Knight, Damon (Ed.), *Turning Points*, Harper & Row, New York, 1977.

Moskowitz, Sam, *Strange Horizons: The Spectrum of Science Fiction* Charles Scribner's Sons, New York, 1976.

Riley, Dick (Ed.), *Critical Encounters: Writers and Themes in Science Fiction*, Frederick Ungar Pub. Co., New York, 1978.

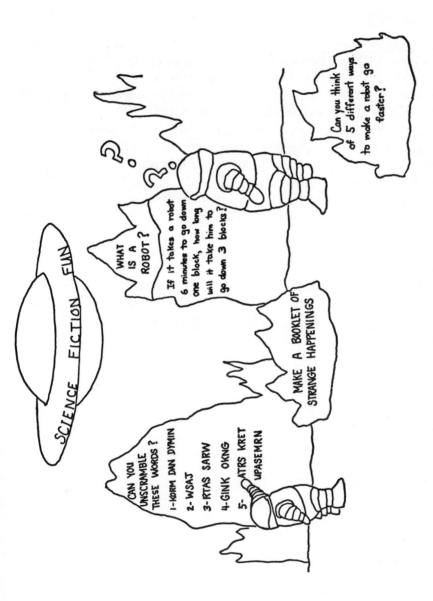

Figure 3-9

Other Related Activities

Language Arts/Science

Issac Asimov wrote stories using a robot theme, basing them on his own "Three Laws of Robotics." What are they? Read one or more of his stories. Find out more about robots. Do they all look the same? Incidentally, try Asimov's nonfiction books for helpful information about astronomy and mathematics. Perhaps you can make up your own story about outer space. Try building a model of a robot using milk and cardboard cartons; if you make his joints loose enough, you can attach strings to this robot's head, hands, and feet to make a marionette.

Read other science fiction stories, such as *The Time Machine, Twenty Thousand Leagues Under the Sea, War of the Worlds,* just to name a few. Where did these stories take place? Make dioramas of some outstanding scenes in these stories. Read more about UFOs, and build models of them. Pretend a space craft really landed on earth. What would happen? Try dramatizing various scenes in a play. Find out about the Loch Ness Monster and make copies of famous pictures showing its head, flipper and back.

4

HOW TO INCREASE LANGUAGE ARTS AND MATH SKILLS

As children learn various basic reading and math skills, they can be challenged to extend this learning to other areas; such as investigating related aspects of science and social studies in stories and poems. Subjects like these *are* good sources of interest and learning. In math, children need not always be limited to work problems. Instead, they may be asked to provide answers to different kinds of problems.

ONE WAY TO COMBINE LANGUAGE ARTS AND CRAFTS: USE STORIES AND POEMS

Crafts are a great way to help improve language and reading skills. Begin with one or two favorite stories and poems with younger children. If you work with older pupils, there's no reason for not taking advantage of longer stories and poems. This means choosing and emphasizing one or more highlights in order, such as certain main events. The rest is up to you.

Another way to use that longer story or poem is by building a learning center from it, or a topic it seems to suggest. Nature studies make a good science topic. Look for others! To do so, use subject areas as starting points. Their interesting backgrounds provide a wealth of material for your class to become involved in. Finally, you may even prefer to pick one especially lively chapter and work from there. Whatever you choose, you may be sure of getting good response from your class.

As you turn various stories and poems into useful language experiences, you are bound to find almost limitless uses for the arts and crafts. Some of these are listed below. For interesting results, use one or more of them in combination.

1. *Figures and dolls* can be made of papier mâché, cardboard, pipecleaners and pebbles. They may represent characters and animals in stories and poems. For example, a painted smooth pebble can be made to look like a lovely frog, on one hand (as in Figure 4-1). Or change its color to red or orange, and you have a ladybird (as in Figure 4-2)! Also you can, use labels to identify the various characters and encourage your class to write other stories and poems from a given character's point of view.

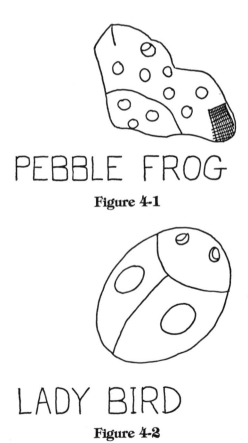

PEBBLE FROG

Figure 4-1

LADY BIRD

Figure 4-2

If children are writing about a caterpillar, how might things look from the ground up? If the story character drives a bus or truck, what are his views about people in general? And his passengers? In order to get a better idea, children should be encouraged to research these occupations, and *then* write.

2. *Puppets* may be made of characters from the story or poem. Besides paper bags, papier mâché and plastic containers, "instant" puppets can be made using pipe-cleaner or cardboard figures. Simply mount the figure on a long strip of cardboard, about 2 × 7 inches, as shown in Figure 4-3. These puppets may be used "as is" or perform on a shoe box stage as in Figure 4-4. While some pupils would enjoy inventing impromptu dialogues,

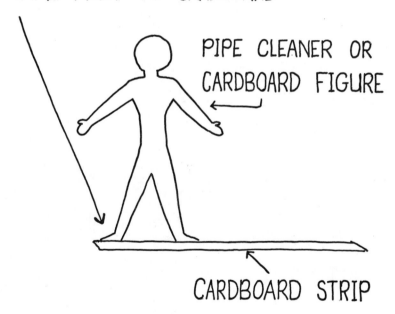

BEND — AND
TAPE FEET TO CARDBOARD

PIPE CLEANER OR
CARDBOARD FIGURE

CARDBOARD STRIP

Figure 4-3

others may prefer writing a puppet play or a monologue based on the story or poem.

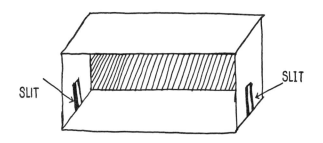

TURN THE SHOE BOX SO THAT THE OPEN SIDE FACES YOU.

A

ONE SIDE OF SHOE BOX

ON BOTH SIDES, CUT A SLIT, ABOUT 3X5, TO ALLOW PUPPETS THROUGH.

B

Figure 4-4

3. *Pictures* can be had from a variety of sources, including old workbooks, coloring books and magazines. Most likely, you will come across a great deal of large and small pictures. Save them! By keeping different pictures in a file, you will be able to provide a variety of language experiences for children. Try the following ideas. Use pictures to:

- Inspire new stories, poems and riddles.
- Make sequence games. That is, cut pictures such as cartoons apart, place them in a box or box lid, and challenge pupils to create new stories from them.

In the meantime, don't overlook childrens' art work. Use childrens' pictures to:

- Make booklets. Here, each booklet could be about one particular topic—dinosaurs, pets, fruits, shells. Have the child write about each picture (based on the story, of course!) Or help him by printing his words underneath. These booklets may be taken home to be read to parents or kept in the classroom library.
- Make book covers based on stories.
- Make one large classroom "story." Children's illustrations of stories can be put to excellent use by arranging such pictures in an orderly sequence— beginning, middle, and end—around the room! Before displaying them, however, have the class write short descriptions under each picture. Once these pictures are up, they will provide a reading experience for each pupil in the class.

4. *Card games* can also be based on a favorite story. Draw pictures or cut them from magazines. Paste a picture on a 3 × 5-inch card and write a question or word about the story underneath. After answering a question correctly, students may win a certain number of points. Pictures may also be matched with words. In order to play any card game, children must read directions and follow rules. Later, they may change these rules if they wish, and write new ones on paper.

5. *Colors* are another resource to use in extending language experiences. For example, an attractive accordion booklet may be made to include the story of what happened when two or three colors were caught in the rain. Still another use of colors is in a game called "Color Me. . . ." Red, for instance, could describe anger, warmth, or even the color of a story character's clothing!

6. *Games* are related to arts and crafts because of their designs, colors, and pictures. They are also related to language art skills because so much reading is involved in understanding directions, naming things, and speaking to classmates. To use games, you need to check your particular story's possibilities: can you relate science, social studies, or math to it? If so, fine! In the meantime, however, you may develop any number of card and board games.

   If you are using the story of *Little Red Riding Hood*, for example, why not include a board game? In Figure 4-5A, the heroine and wolf "race" to Grandma's house. In Figure 4-5B, several paths all lead to Grandma's house in the woods. Which player will reach the house first? To take turns, players use a spinner or dice to progress to Grandma's house. Of course, the player who gets there first is the winner.

   On the other hand, board games may be played by individuals. In such games, a child competes against himself, making more progress as he does so. Begin with a good-sized rectangle of cardboard and divide it into nine 3 × 3-inch squares. After pasting or drawing pictures relating to the story on alternate squares, print a part of the story on the remaining squares. Your game may look something like Figure 4-6.

   On ten 3 × 5-inch cards, write words and draw pictures that correspond to those on the board. To play, the child places the cards face down on the table and draws one card from the top. He then tries to match the card with a corresponding square on the board. When he has finished, he may ask you or another pupil to "check" his board. Or, he can have a classmate competing with him. In that case, whoever uses up all of his or her cards is the winner.

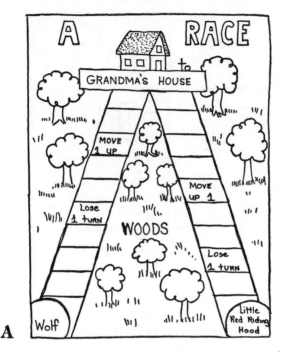

A

B USE SPINNERS - OR DICE

Figure 4-5

Figure 4-6

7. *Dioramas* made of shoe boxes or cardboard cartons may likewise inspire creative writing. Stories, poems, or even songs relating to the scene may be taped to the diorama. Some children may just wish to give a title or oral description of the scene, or turn the whole diorama around and challenge a classmate to name all of the items inside. Whatever the students choose, they will be using language skills creatively.

8. *Puzzles* relating to the given story or poem may be made of pictures. Cut these pictures apart, jigsaw-puzzle style, and place them in a box for pupils to put together. Or cut apart pictures and encourage pupils to talk about what they are doing and describe what is going on as they reconstruct the picture.

AN ACTUAL STORY CENTER
AND HOW TO MAKE IT GROW

General Guidelines

For successful story centers, try choosing a favorite class story, if possible, or try any of the following, for starters:

Snow White and the Seven Dwarfs
The Three Pigs
Aesop's Fables

The Beauty and the Beast
Millions of Cats by Wanda Gag
Ping by Marjorie Flack

Once you've read the story, think of scenes from it that would make good beginnings, middles and endings. Since these scenes will be your center's background, and rather large, aim for simplicity. Instead of showing many trees, for example, show one or two and no more. Then try sketching each one on a scrap of paper. You will have some idea of how the finished scene will look. For a three-dimensional effect, use colored tissue paper or styrofoam to represent parts of trees or buildings.

To give you an idea of the general appearance of such a center, a sketch is included in Figure 4-7. Or, make an "Instant" center from a wooden folding gate, and hang up pictures and various activity cards on its slates. See the sketch in Figure 4-8.

BACKGROUND OF CENTER IS BLACKBOARD
(OR BULLETIN BOARD) SPACE
DIVIDE THIS SPACE INTO 3 EVEN SECTIONS

| PLACE FIRST SCENE OF STORY HERE | PLACE "MIDDLE" PART OF STORY HERE | PLACE LAST PART HERE |

USE TABLE SPACE TO HOLD CHILDRENS' BOOKS, GAMES, ETC.

Figure 4-7

EXAMPLE OF AN INSTANT CENTER

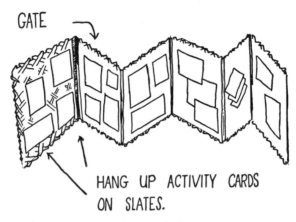

HANG UP ACTIVITY CARDS ON SLATES.

Figure 4-8

During this time, take careful notice of your story's special features. Does its picture of a row of cars, for example, suggest a counting or ordering activity? By all means, use it! You should also consider size (smallest, largest) as well as the colors of cars in the picture. How many blue cars? How many red? Are there more blue cars than yellow ones? How about the cars themselves? Are there more short cars than longer ones?

If it's possible to extend pupils' awareness this way, just think of what can be done with real or mythical animals! Suppose there is a dragon in your story. This time, make a figure of the dragon from papier mâché, milk cartons or a combination of both. Have your class write stories or do dramatizations of it. Children should also investigate legends for more examples of "good" and "bad" dragons.

Getting back to real animals, namely bears, there is just so much you can do with a story like *The Three Bears*, that this center is included as an example.

An Example of a Story Center: "The Three Bears"

First, preliminary sketches were made of beginning, middle, and end scenes from *The Three Bears*. The results are shown in Figure 4-9. In each scene, parts of the story were written on separate pieces of oaktag. Figures were cut out from large pieces of paper and taped to the board. To hold such things as children's work, rulers, activity cards and manila envelopes were taped in appropriate places.

First "background scene" for the story of *The Three Bears*.

Once upon a time, there were 3 bears — the father bear, the mother bear, and of course, baby bear!

Use the rulers to measure this family of bears. How high is the tallest bear? How tall is the mother bear?

What do real bears like to eat? Where do they live?

Write all of the bear facts in a booklet.

One day, the bears went out for a walk in the woods.

What do you enjoy doing when you go on a picnic? Make a list of these things.

A   Figure 4-9

Middle "background scene" from *The Three Bears*.

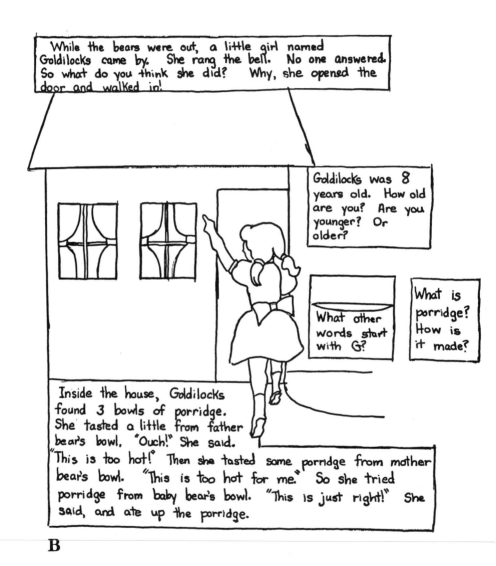

While the bears were out, a little girl named Goldilocks came by. She rang the bell. No one answered. So what do you think she did? Why, she opened the door and walked in!

Goldilocks was 8 years old. How old are you? Are you younger? Or older?

What other words start with G?

What is porridge? How is it made?

Inside the house, Goldilocks found 3 bowls of porridge. She tasted a little from father bear's bowl. "Ouch!" She said. "This is too hot!" Then she tasted some porridge from mother bear's bowl. "This is too hot for me." So she tried porridge from baby bear's bowl. "This is just right!" She said, and ate up the porridge.

B

Figure 4-9 (continued)

Final "background scene" from *The Three Bears*.

Goldilocks was very tired and wanted to sleep. She tried father bear's bed, and said, "Oh, this is too hard!" then she tried mother bear's bed. "Oh dear, this is too soft!" At last, she tried baby bear's bed, and said, "This is just right!" And went to sleep.

Is everything quiet in the forest at night? Read and find out!

Find out how a compass works and learn how to use it.

Show this story in a puppet play.

Pretend that you are Goldilocks. What would you say to your family?

Take a piece of paper and write what they are saying.

What other famous bears do you know about?

When the bears came home, they found an empty bowl of porridge. At first, they didn't see anyone. But they tip-toed in the bedroom. They were very surprised to find a little girl sleeping in baby bear's bed. All of this woke up Goldilocks. She was so scared that she didn't say anything, but ran away as fast as her legs would carry her.

C   Figure 4-9 (continued)

Table Activities for <u>*The Three Bears*</u>

1. Make models of the kitchen, including chairs and bowls. Show sizes "large," "medium" and "small" clearly. Make cardboard dominoes with a picture of large, medium and small bowls, chairs, and beds. Children can match these pictures instead of dots. An example of such a domino is shown in Figure 4-10.

Figure 4-10

2. Make up another story about bears. If you like, use Smokey the Bear or Yogi Bear in your story. Or, write a different ending to the story of *The Three Bears*.

3. Make up a booklet about live bears. How many kinds of bears are there? What do they eat? Where do they live? What else do they do besides hunt? Be sure to look at some of the books about bears in the bibliography.

4. Look at pictures of paw prints made by bears and compare them to those of another animal, such as a dog or cat. How many differences can you notice?

5. Find out what else the word "bear" means.

6. Play slow-moving music, and try to walk like a bear to this music.

7. Make pictures and puppets of other famous bears, such as Smokey and Yogi Bear. You might like to use the pattern of a bear finger puppet picture in Figure 4-11.

Figure 4-11

8. Play "Bear" Category. Find a picture or word that shows something that starts with each of the letters above. Place these pictures and words in the appropriate column as shown in Figure 4-12.

9. Collect enough "bear facts" and make up a guessing game or puzzle of them.

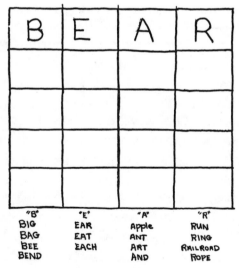

Figure 4-12

10. Collect pictures of bear symbols and make a scrapbook.

11. Add these "bear" words to your list: Paddington, grizzly, den, Teddy Bear, growl, fur, black, brown, sleep, eat, hibernate, cub, honey, winter. Use these words to write a story in a bear booklet, as shown in Figure 4-13.

Figure 4-13

Bibliography of "bear" books

Bamman, Henry, and Whitehead, Robert, *Hunting Grizzly Bears*. Chicago: Benefic Press, 1963.

Bond, Michael, *A Bear Called Paddington*. Houghton Mifflin, 1960.

Byrd, Ernestine, *Ice King*. New York: Scribners, 1965.

Carlson, Natalie, *Alphonse, That Bearded One*. New York: Harcourt, Brace, and World, 1954.

Clark, Ann Nolan, *Bear Cub*. New York: Viking Press, 1965.

Dixon, Paige, *The Young Grizzly*. New York: Atheneum, 1974.

Hancock, Sibyl, *The Grizzly Bear*. Austin, Texas: Steck-Vaughn Co., 1974.

James, Harry, *Grizzly Adams*. Chicago: Children's Press, 1963.

Johnson, Annabel, *The Grizzly*. New York: Harper, 1964.

Liers, Emile, *A Black Bear's Story*. New York: Viking, 1962.

McClung, Robert, *The Mighty Bears*. New York: Random House, 1967.

Mason, George, *The Bear Family*. New York: William Morrow, 1960.

Morey, Walt, *Gentle Ben*. New York: E.P. Dutton, 1965.

Rush, William, *Duff, the Story of a Bear.* New York: Longman, Green, 1950.

Whitehead, Robert. *The First Book of Bears.* New York: Franklin Watts, 1966.

OTHER WAYS TO TELL ABOUT A BOOK

As an alternative to the traditional written book report, give your pupils an opportunity to tell you in their own way about a book they've read. Below are some possible ways:

1. Design a book jacket and write a short description of the book inside.
2. Write an advertisement for the book.
3. Design an accordion-style booklet showing a few highlights of the story.
4. Tell about the book in a poem.
5. Make a puppet character from the story and play "20 Questions" with the other classmates.
6. Make a diorama that includes a scene from the book.
7. Make a classroom mural of the story. Rewrite parts of the story under each picture.
8. Make up a radio or TV dialogue about the book.
9. Make a mask of one of the characters in the story and be a ventriloquist. Discuss the character's part in the book.
10. Be a book critic. Why do you think some parts of the story were uninteresting?
11. Act out one or two scenes from the book.
12. Make up a game based on the story.
13. Make a mobile which includes pictures of the story characters and/or scenes from the book.
14. In one hundred words or less, tell why or why not this book would make a good movie.
15. Take the main character's decision and change it to what *you* would have done instead. What are the results of your actions?

16. Write a letter to one of the characters in the book.

17. If your story is based on history, do some research and find out a bit more about that time. Then write a short essay on the main character's point of view.

18. Write a list of words that would describe this book, then tell about the book using equivalent words.

19. Make a doll representing one of the characters in the story, then describe him in a letter to a friend.

WORKING WITH "DIFFERENT" MATH PROBLEMS

The next time your math lessons include word problems, combine them with open-ended exercises. And be prepared for children do enjoy such problems and often think of ingenious solutions!

Open-ended problems involve several ways in which to find one or more solutions. Although there is almost always some trial-and-error, nothing can beat success in solving a formerly "difficult" problem. True, some of these problems will seem hard to pupils at first. But they are a welcome change from paper and pencil work. Interesting materials, such as Soma cubes, prove to be especially challenging to work with—and are fun besides.

Such cubes nearly always attract children. Originally, they were the invention of Piet Hein, a Danish writer. For a more detailed explanation, try getting a copy of Martin Gardner's fine article entitled "A Game in Which Standard Pieces Composed of Cubes are Assembled into Larger Forms" (*Scientific American*, September, 1958, pp. 182–188). In addition, Gardner includes interesting structures to build in case you would like to try experimenting more on your own.

In each set of cubes, there are seven groups having three or four each. If these groups are arranged in a certain way, different structures may be built, for much depends upon the way a group of cubes is turned and placed. Of all the structures, the large cube is probably the most challenging—and difficult—for pupils to build. Moreover, there are many, many ways to build a single cube.

Some Guidelines

Although other sources suggest the use of sugar cubes to make this puzzle, wooden blocks are by far the easiest to obtain and handle. To make a set, you will need 27 of these blocks and strong glue. Make each group of cubes by looking at the diagrams in Figure 4-14 for positions. Glue the blocks in these positions and allow ample drying time. If you allow yourself time to experiment with the Soma cube before introducing it to your class, you will have a much better idea of how to use the cube with children.

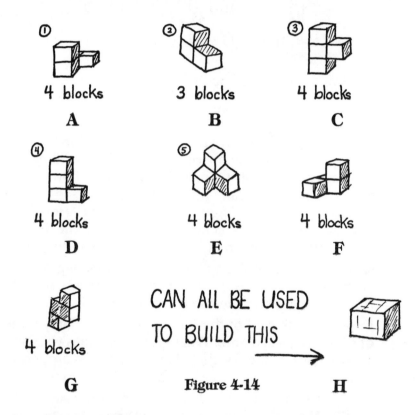

Figure 4-14

One Way to Begin

If Soma cubes are new to your class, you may prefer to introduce them to one or two groups of pupils at a time. Or, include the puzzle as part of your math enrichment center. Allow some time for experimentation, and after the children have had this initial introduction, use the following suggestions on accompanying activity cards:

Activities

1. Add more blocks to the structure pictured below, and "make something out of it." Try to build three different things.

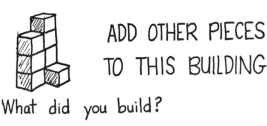

ADD OTHER PIECES
TO THIS BUILDING

What did you build?

Figure 4-15

2. Try building a cube. If you are doing this for the first time, give yourself plenty of time. Then try building the cube again. Only this time, keep a record of how long it took you to do it. Can you build it in less time? Use a different way of building the cube each time. How long does it take? Try this activity with a friend and have a contest to see who can build a cube in the shortest time.

3. First build a cube. Then make it into something else by taking away some pieces and/or changing others around. How many different items can you make this way?

4. Instead of using all of the puzzle pieces, use only three or four groups at a time. What groups of cubes will form an even rectangle? Try changing these pieces around to make an animal. Invent an animal, this time, if you wish.

5. Directions to teachers: Build a cube, using all of the blocks. Next, find a picture of a face in a magazine and cut it out. Paste the picture against one side of your cube. Then "slice" the picture apart at the seams where the cubes meet. The object of this activity is to build the cube and still have the pieces correctly show the face on one side. It's harder than it looks! Challenge pupils to "build a face."

6. Instead of using a face, paste or glue colored paper to one side of the completed cube, again, slicing apart at the seams formed where the cubes meet. Instead of using only one side of the cube, use a different color on each of the four sides. Have pupils build the cube, making sure that all four sides show the band of color.

7. No cubes are necessary for this activity, only the experience of using them. On separate 3 × 5-inch cards, draw one or two groups of puzzle cubes. Try drawing some of the pieces from another point of view. Make up about 25 to 35 cards. Pupils should try to "build" (or imagine) different structures by placing two or more cards together. Then try to build these items using the actual puzzle. This activity gives children practice in visualization.

8. Soma cubes can provide the beginnings of a "Math Puzzle Center." (See Figure 4-16.) Make up a giant maze for the background of this center on a large piece of wrapping paper. Besides Soma cubes, include paper-and-pencil "brainteasers," wire puzzles, and mazes. One special feature of this center may also include "the puzzle of the day—can you solve it?"

Figure 4-16

MAKING MULTI-PURPOSE ARITHMETIC AIDS

To get the variety in math that you need on short notice, you may wish to consider aids which are multi-purpose. That is, the same item need not be made separately each time a change is desired; you only need to substitute the new in place of the old on the aid itself. In the end, you will have more time to work with a greater number of individual pupils and still provide the ways and means to motivate practice in arithmetic skills.

1. *All-purpose drill cube.* Enlarge and use the pattern in Figure 4-17 to make a two-inch cardboard cube. With adhesive tape, attach practice examples on separate slips of paper to each side of the cube. These examples may include addition, subtraction, multiplication and division. Players then take turns in tossing the cube and answering the examples that come up. To use this cube again, remove the old tape and paper slips. Make a set of new slips and tape them to each side of the cube.

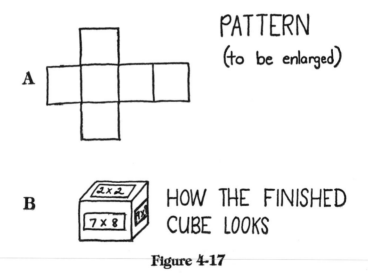

A

PATTERN
(to be enlarged)

B   HOW THE FINISHED
CUBE LOOKS

Figure 4-17

2. Try a different number line—one with tabs—to help make counting easier. Each tab represents a point to be counted and thus helps eliminate confusion. To make

this desk number line, divide a strip of 1 × 22-inch cardboard or oaktag into 12 sections. Write a number from one to twelve in each section, then cut twelve 1 × ¼-inch construction paper slips and paste a strip over each line, leaving about a ½-inch at the top, as shown in Figure 4-18.

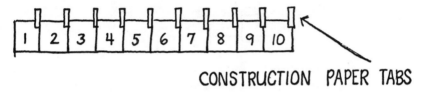

CONSTRUCTION PAPER TABS

Figure 4-18

3. *Spin-a-Problem.* This aid may be used by one or more pupils. To make it, draw a large circle on an 8½ × 11-inch piece of cardboard. Make an inner circle, and divide the space between these circles into about nine equal sections. On corresponding pieces of adhesive tape, write practice addition, subtraction, multiplication or division examples. Find the middle of the circle and mark it with a tiny hole. Cut out an arrow from a smaller piece of cardboard, push a paper fastener through it, and attach everything to the center of the circle. To use this aid, the child lets the arrow spin and tries to answer whatever problem it points to. He gets one point for each correct answer. (See Figure 4-19.)

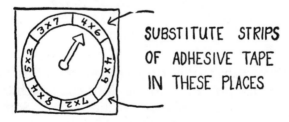

SUBSTITUTE STRIPS
OF ADHESIVE TAPE
IN THESE PLACES

Figure 4-19

4. *Juice can jamboree.* To begin with, save all sizes of juice cans. Then use them to make the following aids:

Numeral cans. Tape a construction paper number to each juice can, from 1 to 20. (See Figure 4-20.) Mix cans up. Now have pupils put them in order. In addition, a corresponding number of ice cream sticks may be placed in each can to reinforce the idea of the number.

Figure 4-20

Juice can place-holder. Want children to have a better idea of hundred's, ten's, and one's places? Use a tall juice can and label it "100's." Label the next tallest juice can "10's," and the smallest one as "1's." Cut out corresponding holes at the bottom of a box, turn this box upside-down and place the cans inside, in order. Now write numbers such as "359" on each of about 20 index cards. Have pupils place the correct number of sticks in each place-holder can. (See Figure 4-21.)

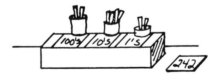

Figure 4-21

5. Use juice cans to describe figures. To do this, place juice cans in key positions on the floor and attach the correct lengths of string or cord to these cans. Some sample figures are shown in Figure 4-22. Juice cans are good sources of story problems. On each can, for example, the amount of concentrated juice is measured in the metric, as well as in our own system. Prices are also

stamped on each can. Use these cans to make up problems for pupils to solve. Children can also try measuring
the length of cans and comparing sizes. Having done
this, they will have enough information to discover if
that brand is a good buy for their needs. To help get this
idea across, substitute a hypothetical family of four.
Given this information, what size and brand of juice
would be the best buy for this family? Suppose this family finds a coupon in the newspaper that is worth twenty
cents off for two cans of Brand X juice. Is this coupon
worth using or not? Why?

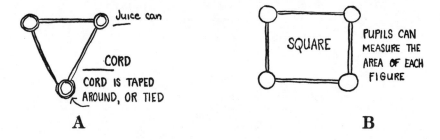

Figure 4-22

5

STRATEGIES
FOR MAKING THE MOST
OF HOLIDAY THEMES

As you know, children have much to look forward to before and during the holidays. There is usually time off from school, and most of all, there is a lot of excitement, fun and festivities. During these special days, children also have many opportunities to learn about different traditions, crafts and culture. But some of the lesser-known holidays may offer interesting historical sidelights as well. For example, Johnny Appleseed Chapman's birthday falls on September 26, and can be commemorated with related activities in folklore, social studies, art and science. Or, perhaps it can be related in some way to one or more present class units.

Most of the time, you will find it helpful to keep special days like this in mind by including them on a large class calendar and drawing on them as handy sources to enrich all areas of the curriculum. Such days also provide additional information and material for pupils to read and think about. Of course this is only a sample of what can be done. Later on in this chapter, you will find a variety of helpful hints for practically all the holidays, as well as ways of making the excitement of special days work for you.

A. WAYS TO HAVE HASSLE-FREE HOLIDAYS

While it is true that you will always have some last-minute details to handle as holidays arrive, there are ways to ease much of the confusion.

Probably the best way is by allowing yourself plenty of time, say four or five weeks, *before* a particular holiday. Jotting down everything, from the most important to the smallest detail on a calendar will help too. As tempting as putting off those smaller details seems, don't! If you do, you will find that such details will have to be crowded into an already tight schedule.

First, find a place on the calendar for items that should be done soon. This includes locating and sending for materials, and making and preparing others. Use the first week or so to complete these details. In the following weeks, schedule those things that are somewhat less urgent, but must be done nevertheless. Begin slowly. Try for a goal of two or three completed items per week. Start other projects only after these are done, and by the time that holiday week arrives, you will be well prepared. Below are more timesavers.

1. Make or obtain a large calendar and post it nearby.

2. Look for ways to save money. Whenever possible, use junk materials and/or recycle last year's items instead of buying commercial ones.

3. Keep each holiday idea on separate 3 × 5-inch cards on your desk in a handy file. In addition to typical ideas for specific holidays, include categories for greeting cards, bulletin boards, activities, and class management.

4. Check children's books for information about related holidays, crafts, stories, and pictures *first*. These sources will help you cut your preparation time in half.

5. Choose more activities that allow children to work independently or with a buddy.

6. If you teach kindergarten or any of the primary grades, have children decorate their own "take-home" bags a day or two before the big holiday.

7. To help identify children's projects quickly, have pupils initial their things in advance.

8. Provide craft activities that are simple yet can be done within a reasonable time. Or at least choose those activities which allow children to see results.

9. Put away the "old" materials and novelties children have become accustomed to using and introduce the "new," a little at a time.

10. Allow all pupils to participate in helping out for the holidays. To make things easier, let helpers know when they will be needed in advance, and make a list of those pupils.

11. If you wish to give a single item away and want to do it in the fairest way possible, select a number, write it on a slip and set aside. Then, ask children to tell you a number they have chosen from one to ten or one or twenty. The child who chooses the "lucky number" wins the item, fair and square!

B. HOW TO USE SPECIAL DAYS TO THE BEST ADVANTAGE

1. Look for ways to use popular *and* lesser-known holidays as starting points for other areas of the curriculum.

2. For future use, take Polaroid® pictures of bulletin boards and/or classroom activities you thought were especially effective.

3. Challenge pupils to build or make something different using so-called "holiday colors" and/or materials.

4. Make good use of themes such as "How Holidays Have Changed." For example, how was Christmas celebrated in 1775? 1875? 1975?

5. Teach a quiet craft such as sewing or weaving to pupils for those in-between days during a holiday season.

6. Have pupils find out how various ethnic groups celebrate the same holiday. Through related crafts and decorations, the children will gain a better understanding of different peoples.

7. Encourage pupils to use their own ingenuity in illustrating holiday symbols, pictures, festivities and the like.

8. You may also find that using the month during which one or more holidays occur allows some leeway for exploring interesting aspects of those days.

To make any holiday special, take a look at it from "behind the scenes" to see what it has to offer. For starters, make a list of symbols and customs associated with a given holiday; then try extending them a bit. Are any symbols and/or customs linked at all to seasons and changing weather, a particular month, traditions and legends? Combine these with other areas of the curriculum in addition to art and social studies—science, math, language arts, physical education and music. In science, for example, draw on related aspects of conservation, astronomy or ecology. Add a different dimension to social studies by having pupils find out what the first train, plane or newspaper was like. What was it called in those times? What did it look like? How did it work at first? What made it seem especially appropriate for that period of time? How did people react to it?

On the other hand, you might wish to emphasize a certain curriculum area, or build a theme from it. Try extending this theme. To do this, see the first part of Chapter 3 for suggestions. Additional ways to help make *any* holiday special include the following:

1. Make life-size figures by stuffing paper bags and/or used clothing in them and placing them in a giant diorama. For example, pose these figures in a scene from a holiday-related story or even a celebration in a foreign land. Figures may be placed or painted in a refrigerator carton or a box from another large appliance.

2. Make holiday-related mobiles. In addition to using wire hangers, bend corrugated cardboard strips to form foundations for mobiles. Then hang cardboard or small models of holiday letters, words or pictures.

3. Make and use masks for holidays other than Halloween, for example. Experiment with cardboard cartons for

larger masks. Some characters you may wish to try making include Uncle Sam, Johnny Appleseed, Betsy Ross and Christopher Columbus.

4. Take advantage of holiday names in bingo games by including only those letters and pictures having to do with the holiday names. In the word "Christmas," for example, related words beginning with "C" are candle, cards, cold, chimney, and carols; for "H," try words like holly or hat; "R" words might be ring and reindeer, "I" may stand for ice and icicle, while "S" may include snowmen, sled, shop, stores, stars, scarf, and snow. For "T," use words like tree, tops, and toys, for "M" use merry, mittens and mistletoe, for "A" use antlers and for "S" snowflakes, etc. On each bingo card, write words in some spaces and draw or paste pictures in the remaining spaces. Then write the names of these items on separate slips of paper and play this game in the usual way.

5. Make a "Holiday Book" as a class project for a given holiday. Include examples of pupil stories, poems, and pictures, as well as polaroid photos of children's activities. Place this book in your class library as an extra special feature for a week or so after the holiday. Use it as a source for language experiences and later on as a holiday idea-book for next year.

6. Emphasize the next holiday by making and using a giant greeting card to hold related activity cards and/or greeting cards. To make, simply cut a refrigerator or television carton as shown in Figure 5-1. Paint the inner part of the carton with a suitable pastel color of your choice. After allowing some drying time, you may wish to coat the painted interior with shellac. Decorate the interior with holiday-related language and art activity cards, or use the giant card as a display for pupils' handmade greeting cards.

In addition to a display, these refrigerator boxes make fine stage props for class plays. You can, for exam-

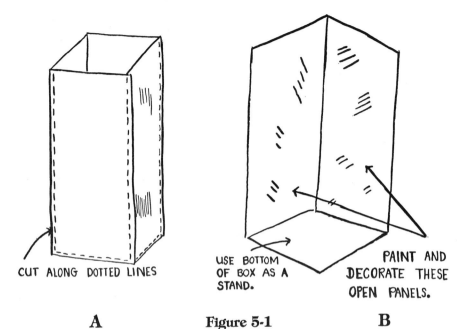

CUT ALONG DOTTED LINES

USE BOTTOM OF BOX AS A STAND.

PAINT AND DECORATE THESE OPEN PANELS.

A Figure 5-1 **B**

ple, cut large figure outlines of people and/or animals. Use the bottom of the carton as a foundation, or make another foundation from a smaller carton. An example of this is given in Figure 5-2.

7. Take advantage of holidays as further opportunities to increase understanding, awareness and appreciation of other cultures. Try making craft items and if possible, experiment with native recipes.

C. A SHORT GUIDE TO SPECIAL DAYS AND ACTIVITIES

In addition to these and other ideas to give each holiday a new look, try extending familiar symbols. What else do their designs or colors seem to suggest? In what ways can these symbols be used to give children new perspectives on a particular holiday? How about related reading and math skills?

LARGE FIGURE

PLACE FIGURE IN SLIT
OF SMALLER CARTON, OR
TAPE IT TO THE STAND

SMALLER CARTON

Figure 5-2

Still another way of giving a holiday a "new look" is by making use of seasonal activities. For example, you will most likely read or hear about harvests during the Halloween and Thanksgiving holidays, and how farmers protected their cornfields with scarecrows. From the simplest to the most elaborate, these scarecrows were sometimes works of art, and some further consideration might be given to such figures as art forms. Disguises, different types of masks, and stories behind them are interesting, related topics. Other examples of a few popular and lesser-known special days, along with possible "starting points" for activities follow.

Month: September

Significance (special meaning, holidays): the end of summer vacation and the beginning of school, beginning of autumn.

Holidays and special days: Labor Day, Citizenship Day, American Indian Day (fourth Friday in September), Rosh Hashanah, National Hispanic Heritage Week, Good Neighbor Day, Johnny Appleseed Chapman's Birthday, Responsible Pet-Care Week.

Activities:

American Indian Day. This is an excellent time to take another look at various stereotypes of Indians—wigwams, headdresses, and attitudes depicting Indians as the "bad guys." Did all Indians live or dress this way? On a large piece of wrapping paper, draw a map of the United States and use a color code to designate the locations of former and present Indian tribes. If possible, try finding and pasting pictures of the different kinds of homes Indians made for themselves. How did they use the environment? Who were some famous "real life" Indians? How are they different from such fictional Indians as Hiawatha or Tonto? What tribes of Indians live or lived in your state? Take a survey of towns, lakes, rivers and other places with Indian names. What do those names mean?

National Hispanic Heritage Week. Learn Spanish words for "Hello," "good-bye," "good morning" and "good night." Make a bulletin board of Spanish explorers or heroes. Explore various

LARGE MAP OF
SOUTH AMERICA

DOLLS FOR EACH
COUNTRY

DISPLAY TRAVEL FOLDERS ABOUT EACH
COUNTRY ON EACH SIDE

Figure 5-3

dramatic possibilities in Cervantes' *Don Quixote,* such as the windmill scene. Learn about a typical day in the life of a South American child. Make a set of dolls to represent each South and Central American country and include them in a bulletin board such as the one pictured in Figure 5-3. Or, focus on one particular country and develop a theme around it, such as "Chile—Through a Camera's Eye" or "Mexico—Yesterday and Today." Display travel folders obtained from your local agency, or ones you have made yourself on the bulletin board. Explore various myths and legends related to ancient stone monuments.

Good Neighbor Day. On one hand, try placing focus on the world communities as good neighbors by way of the values all peoples share as well as similarities among foreign languages, etc. This can also be done with folk tales; although some plots are familiar, each culture has made a story its own by including its values, customs, etc. For suggestions on how to use folk tales, see Chapter 7.

You can also collect cartoons about neighbors. Have you ever been in a similar situation? In what way was it different from the one in the cartoon? In what way was it similar? Make

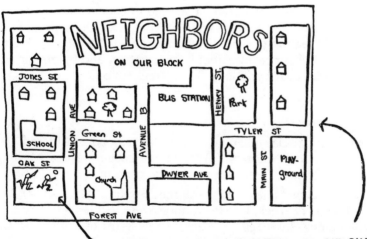

ATTACH CUT-OUT FIGURES OF NEIGHBORS
DOING THINGS, SUCH AS GOING TO
SCHOOL, THROWING A FRISBEE, ETC.

Figure 5-4

a booklet or display of particularly humorous incidents from these cartoons. Invent your own cartoons or comic book heroes and heroines; organize them around various themes, such as "How We Help Each Other" or "Good Times We Share." Make a bulletin board, such as the one pictured in Figure 5-4, depicting an urban or suburban scene and taping on cut-outs of neighbors relaxing, chattering, working, reading, jogging, etc.

Johnny Appleseed Chapman's Birthday. (September 26th) Celebrate this day by reading the story of Johnny Appleseed (Yes, he *was* a real person!) and taking advantage of a possible unit about good health, seeds, and planting. Johnny Appleseed also urged people to plant trees and be aware of conservation as well. There are also different varieties of apples, such as Red Delicious, Golden Delicious, McIntosh, Rome Beauty, and so on. What do they look like? Just for fun, try planting an apple seed. Get recipes for making or sample apple pie, apple cider, and apple butter. Make applehead dolls. Make apple pendants. There are several ways of doing this: cut an apple shape from cardboard, felt, or the lid of a small box. To model such an apple, try using Play-Doh, or papier-mâché. Then attach a string to the top, either in a paper-clip hook you have already inserted or a hole you have made for that purpose—and your pendant is complete. Other projects include learning about the names and types of well-known trees in your region, about conservation, and by preparing a bulletin board entitled, "How Trees Help Us."

Month: October

Significance (special meaning, holidays): may be considered "the month of explorers." Weather is cooler, leaves begin to change color in some parts of the country.

Holidays and special days: Yom Kippur, Sputnik Day (Oct. 4), National Pet Week, Fire Prevention Week, National Poetry Day, National Joke Telling Week, Anniversary of *Robert Goddard*, rocket-builder (Oct. 19) who also predicted that we would be able to travel to Mars, UN Day (Oct. 24), *Leif Erikson Day*, (Oct. 9), *Columbus Day* (Oct. 12), Halloween (Oct. 31) and the celebration of National Magic Day, honoring the death of Houdini in 1926.

Activities:

National Pet Week. How do you take care of *your* pet, especially during very cold or very hot weather? Make a chart showing ways to care for dogs, cats, gerbils, fish, etc. Learn something about a career working with animals—what does a veterinarian do? Make a list of fictional pets you may have seen on TV or heard about, such as Mr. Ed, Black Beauty, Kermit the Frog, Mickey Mouse, Donald Duck or Kliban's Cats. Classify these animals according to: those who have fur or feathers, those who don't, by color, by number and kinds of feet, and by diet. What are real horses, frogs, mice, ducks or cats like? In what ways do they communicate with you, with other animals whether friend or foe? Invent other make-believe animals; make puppets. Learn about pet shelters and what kinds of jobs are available. Have a pet show, using·real or make-believe pets made of paper, cardboard, or cloth. Give a prize to the largest, smallest, longest, shortest, funniest, and most photogenic pets. Make a list of every word you can think of that describes your pet. Make up stories about your or someone else's pet, Kipling-style, such as why cats like fish, why frogs hop. Make pet calendars, using a different pet for each month, and explain why you chose that pet. Include all of these things in a "Pet Booklet" along with nursery rhymes about pets, information about animal sounds and what kind of pet you would like to own and why.

National Poetry Day. Find poems that are related to your environment including pets, sounds, colors, buildings. Experiment with similar poems you have invented. Find stories that contain rhyming words, like those in Dr. Seuss's books. Experiment with different kinds of rhymes and include them in a "rhyme booklet." Make up a game, based on a rhyme. Make a display or bulletin board around "the poem of the week" or "the poem of the month."

National Joke Telling Week. See suggestions for April Fool's Day. Think up as many varieties of the "knock-knock" jokes as you can. Learn about and use puns. Tell about a joke that was played on you; how did you feel? What is your version of a good sport? Describe it in writing by satire, or make a model of a good sport. Try using this word as a pun. Did you ever have a joke that backfired—if so, what happened? Was it still funny afterwards? A long time ago, a person who entertained royalty was known as a "jester." Did these people do anything else? Look for books about the Middle Ages and try to find information about jesters.

UN Day. Make models of the craft specialties of various nations in the UN and put them on a class display. Make a large chart showing the different organizations of the UN. Read the latest news on the UN. What are some problems? In what ways has progress been made? Have a debate on one or both of these questions. Make miniature flags of UN nations and display them.

Leif Erikson Day. Leif Erikson is also credited with discovering a part of America, about 500 years before Columbus. He sailed from Greenland to the part of Canada known as Newfoundland. Use this day to find out more about the Vikings. What did their boats look like? Why did they sail at such distances? What were some of their legends? Use a map to trace Erikson's route from Greenland to Newfoundland. Make up a play about Erikson going off on this expedition.

Columbus Day. Extend a few usual activities by learning more about using a compass. Try making a simple one. At first, it was thought that the earth was flat and monsters of all kinds waited at the edge of the earth. Use your imagination to include them in various dioramas. Find stories and pictures of the Loch Ness Monster. What kinds of animals look like monsters; make models of them, print descriptions of them on separate cards, and use them to form a classroom "zoo." Who are some of our so-called "modern day" explorers? Read about pirates and locate some of their hiding places on a map. Who were the famous pirates, both in real life and in fiction? Make dolls and pose them in their probable settings using a large box lid as a foundation for a painted setting. What might have been in a treasure chest besides gold coins? Using today's standards of monetary value, make a list of possible items in a treasure chest along with the value of each item and tell what that chest would be worth. In a model chest, include what people today would most likely fight for besides money. What do you think modern explorers need to know in finding out about a strange land—or planet? It might help to picture yourself in a strange city, perhaps one from science fiction, and figure out what you would do first. How would you get around.?

Some fictional explorers worth reading about include *Gulliver's Travels, Alice in Wonderland, Jason and the Argonauts* and *Robinson Crusoe*. All of these have excellent dramatization possibilities. Or, better yet, include memorable scenes for a bulletin board entitled, "October—Month of Explorers."

Halloween. Read such Halloween-related stories as *The Legend of Sleepy Hollow* and *George the Ghost*. Using pipe cleaners, scrap wire, or twigs, add finishing touches to make miniature scarecrows. Have fun with masks by giving some kind of small prize for the following categories: masks with the least amount of materials, masks with unusual combinations of materials, different types of happy and sad masks. Learn to do simple magic tricks. Try making up directions explaining how to do one of these tricks and have a friend perform the trick, doing exactly the things you suggest. Science-related "magic" may also include experiments with disappearing ink. Because Halloween and National Magic Day occur at the same time, these activities are quite appropriate. This is also a good time to read about famous magicians, such as Houdini. Take an inventory of the kinds of tricks they did.

Remember that orange, yellow and brown are associated with autumn and the harvest in particular. Use these colors to make autumn designs in crayon resist, cardboard stencils, Halloween motifs, etc. Make a collage of autumn fruits such as apples, and vegetables such as corn and pumpkins. Learn legends about these plants. What did the Indians, for example, believe about certain vegetables such as corn?

Month: November

Significance (special meaning, holidays): First Automobile Show (Nov. 3, 1900); Election Day; Veteran's Day; Anniversary of Edison's first "talking machine" (Nov. 21, 1877); Thanksgiving Day; November 30th: birthday of Churchill, Mark Twain and Jonathan Swift.

Activities:

First Automobile Show. Find pictures of cars that were owned in the early 1900's. How were they run? What did the older electric cars look like? How did people dress, play and work in those days? Use a picture or microfilm of a typical newspaper from those times. Make posters advertising a possible "auto show" of 1910 or another suitable date. What would be included that might not be seen in our modern auto shows? Make models of older cars using cardboard, shoe boxes, cardboard tubes, and papier mâché. Write a dialogue that might have been made by a newscaster in advertising this show. What other inventions were made available to people during the early 1900's? Make up a poem or song about them, incorporating sounds they made.

Anniversary of Edison's First "Talking Machine." Find out what such a machine looked like. Before the telephone was invented, how did people communicate? Make up something you would have said if you were the first person to use this talking machine. Draw cartoons of people in various occupations using this machine for the first time, including some of the things they might have said. Pretend that it is possible for Edison to visit you. Take him on a tour of inventions that were made after his time and make up a dialogue of this event. Put yourself in an inventor's place by pretending that you are trying to invent a cheaper, more efficient means of land transportation. What are some of the things you would have to take into consideration? Suppose your invention was an overnight success. Would you continue to work this way? Explain what you would do.

Thanksgiving Day. Thanksgiving Day is actually a very old holiday, for the Mayans celebrated it with a large feast and similar ball games. Read about the way in which the ancient Greeks and Romans celebrated their versions of Thanksgiving. Make up a story about a celebration that might have taken place.

Using paper bags, make figures of turkeys, Pilgrims, Indians and perhaps a large Horn of Plenty. (See Figure 5-5.) Use these stuffed paper bag figures as room decorations. In addition to traditional figures, try making a family—father, mother and child—and "seat" them at a table for Thanksgiving. Attach strong black thread or fishing line to figures and hang in the classroom.

Mark Twain's Birthday (Nov. 30). Celebrate this great writer's birthday by reading some of the adventures of Tom Sawyer. Make figures of Tom Sawyer and Huckleberry Finn and place them in appropriate settings, such as a table or carton with a painted background. What was life like during those times? Pretend you were a child then; how would you amuse yourself? What would you learn in school? Make a large Mark

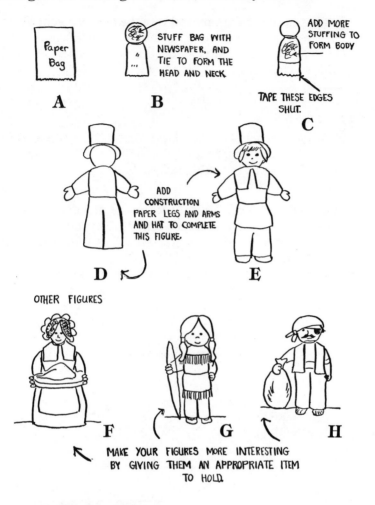

A

Paper Bag

B

STUFF BAG WITH NEWSPAPER, AND TIE TO FORM THE HEAD AND NECK.

C

ADD MORE STUFFING TO FORM BODY

TAPE THESE EDGES SHUT.

D

ADD CONSTRUCTION PAPER LEGS AND ARMS AND HAT TO COMPLETE THIS FIGURE.

E

OTHER FIGURES

F   G   H

MAKE YOUR FIGURES MORE INTERESTING BY GIVING THEM AN APPROPRIATE ITEM TO HOLD.

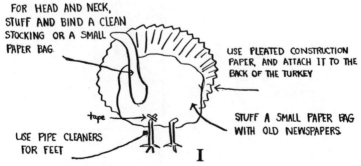

FOR HEAD AND NECK, STUFF AND BIND A CLEAN STOCKING OR A SMALL PAPER BAG.

USE PLEATED CONSTRUCTION PAPER, AND ATTACH IT TO THE BACK OF THE TURKEY

tape

STUFF A SMALL PAPER BAG WITH OLD NEWSPAPERS.

USE PIPE CLEANERS FOR FEET

I

Figure 5-5

Twain puppet or dummy and take the part of a ventriloquist. Exchange humorous stories or have a serious conversation. Have Mark Twain answer questions about his life and/or work in your class.

Month: December

Significance (special meaning, holidays): Dec. 2, 1927, Model A Ford was introduced, costing $385; December 16, 1773, Boston Tea Party; Christmas Day; Hanukkah.

Activities:

Christmas and *Hanukkah,* December's major holidays, are celebrated with a variety of related activities. In addition to these, try enhancing the winter season as well as these special days with the following ideas:

1. Include a science unit about sounds entitled "Festival of Sounds." Listen to sounds at this time of the year in school, in the street, in stores and at home. Experiment with sound by tying a string to a ping pong ball and attach it to the inside of a cardboard carton, as shown in Figure 5-6. Try hitting the ball against the sides and back of the box. What kind of sounds are made? Make or identify other sounds such as bells, clocks, timers, xylophone, keys, balloons and rubber bands. Find instructions in various children's books about how to make and use musical instruments.

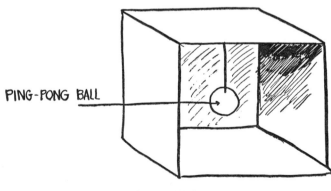

PING-PONG BALL

Figure 5-6

2. Make simple toys that move, particularly certain kinds of science toys. Find out what makes them work. Instructions for these can be obtained from children's books about physics and physics experiments. At a later time, display these toys and include short description cards that tell what scientific principles are involved as well as an interesting fact or two. A study of these toys could lead to a short unit on shopping and comparing prices, and what makes certain kinds of toys worth buying more than others.
3. Use paper folding to create various figures. During your first few attempts, practice with scrap paper and simply made objects. Gradually try enlarging these items as well as using different types of paper.

Month: January

Holidays and special days: New Year's Day; Chinese New Year's Festival (fifteen days beginning in late January or early February); Dr. Martin Luther King's Birthday; National Education Week on Smoking; National Boat Show; first real atomic submarine, *Nautilus,* launched from Groton, Ct. on January 21, 1954; first U.S. satellite launched on January 31, 1958.

Activities:

New Year's Day (and celebrations). The beginning of a new year is not always celebrated at the same time or in the same way. The Chinese, for example, name each year for an animal and celebrate with a big parade. Make up a humorous booklet entitled "Ten Ways to Get Rid of the Old Year Besides Forgetting It." In other words, how could those resolutions be kept track of and *kept,* for a change? Name every way you can think of. Make masks and lanterns of many kinds. Find out how ancient cultures celebrated their own "new year." Use this time to learn more about old and new calendars.

National Education Week on Smoking. Make posters; find out what lungs look like after being exposed to constant smoking and related diseases. Find other ways to stay in shape, such as running and jogging. Investigate other types of air pollution and what is being done about it, such as anti-pollution devices on autos. Make up puppet plays and cartoons about why it isn't such a good idea to smoke in the first place. Collect cigarette advertisements from newspapers and magazines and underline words and sentences used to convince people to buy cigarettes or why smoking is such fun. Make up a dialogue about a doctor and a person who is beginning to smoke and likes it. Think of arguments for both sides, or debate this question in class.

National Boat Show. Boats were among the first forms of transportation. Make a catalog of famous boats, such as the *Mayflower, Pinta, Nina, Santa Maria* and the *Queen Mary.* Find pictures of these boats. Relate this information to submarines. Read and dramatize parts of such stories as Jules Verne's *Twenty Thousand Leagues Under the Sea.* Make up your own science fiction stories about the sea, fish, sailors or pirates. As you write, try reversing the circumstances. This time, make man or his counterpart the villain instead of the fish. Change the date to about the year 3000, and describe what happens.

Month: February

Holidays and special days: Ground Hog Day; Lincoln's Birthday; Washington's Birthday; Brotherhood Week (celebrated the same time as Lincoln's birthday); Valentine's Day; Mardi Gras; first public school (Feb. 13); Negro History Week and Frederick Douglas's Birthday (Feb. 12–14).

Activities:

Lincoln's Birthday. Look at pictures of how Lincoln was portrayed—on a penny or in Gutzon Borglum's famous sculpture at Mt. Rushmore in South Dakota. Find out more about this sculpture and make your own model of it. Read Sandburg's account of Lincoln's boyhood. Build a model of a log cabin, using Lincoln Logs. Make stamps honoring Lincoln. Read Lincoln's humorous stories and speeches.

St. Valentine's Day. Make, enlarge and/or exaggerate valentine shapes in Figure 5-7. Use construction paper, wire, plastic straws or rolled-up newspapers. Some of these valentines may even serve as mobiles, as shown in Figure 5-8. Find out what other shapes are symmetrical besides the valentine heart. In addition to cutting paper in these different forms, try folding a piece of paper in half and placing a drop of red

Figure 5-7

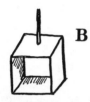
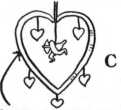

USE ENVELOPE AND OTHER KINDS OF BOXES TO MAKE 3-D VALENTINE CARDS. THEN CUT OR PASTE A MOTIF OR MESSAGE ON EACH SIDE. THESE "CARDS" MAY ALSO SERVE AS MOBILES.

ROLLED-UP NEWSPAPER FORMS VALENTINE AND OUTLINE OF MOBILE. USE BLACK OR NAVY-BLUE THREAD TO HANG VARIOUS MOTIFS.

OR

USE THE WORD "LOVE" TO MAKE MOBILES. FIRST, WRITE THE WORD IN AS MANY POSSIBLE WAYS AS YOU CAN. USE FELT, CARDBOARD OR ROLLED-UP NEWS-PAPERS FOR LETTERS.

Figure 5-8

ink or paint in the center. Fold the paper again and open it up. What happened? Or use these other symmetrical shapes to decorate bookcovers, or make mobiles and paper puppet heads.

Is a real human heart symmetrical? Look at line drawings of a human heart. Using these drawings as inspiration, make line drawings of different kinds of hearts such as the kinds that might be "found" in make-believe robots, Superman or a world-famous athlete of your choice, etc. Use the word "heart" in messages for Valentine's Day, such as "You have my heart on a string," and draw on paper what these messages "literally" may mean. Perhaps one or more of such drawings may be used on the front cover of a Valentine's Day card.

Read and dramatize legends associated with this day and/or its symbols.

Month: March

Holidays and special days: (Japanese) Girls' Doll Festival (Mar. 3rd); National Peanut Month; Aunt's Day (Mar. 8th); "Uncle Sam's" Birthday (Mar. 13); First American horror film (Mar. 18); National Wildlife Week; Amerigo Vespucci's Birthday (Mar. 9); Houdini's Birthday; Youth Art Month; Save Your Vision Week; Roentgen's Birthday, the German scientist who discovered X-rays (Mar. 27); St. Patrick's Day.

Activities:

Uncle Sam's Birthday. Look at cartoons of Uncle Sam in past and present political cartoons and posters: what were the "signs of the times?" Draw your own version of Uncle Sam. Make masks in papier mâché or paper bags. Find other symbols that stand for the United States. Find out what symbols are used to represent Britain and Russia. Make up possible slogans Uncle Sam might use today and draw them on posters. Uncle Sam was a real person: read a book about him and report on it to the class. Collect cartoons pertaining to Uncle Sam from newspapers and magazines, and place them in a scrapbook. Write an essay or speech that Uncle Sam might give about America's advantages despite hard times.

First American horror film. Make masks of favorite horror-film creatures such as the Frankenstein monster, King Kong, Wolfman or Dracula. Make these masks seem as life-like as possible, or better yet, exaggerate certain characteristics to make them futuristic. Look at photographs of still lifes from various films and see the effective use made of black-and-white photography, stage design, outdoor settings, action shots, etc. Experiment with animation using line drawings of horror film favorites. Find out how Mary Shelley came to write *Frankenstein*. If the Frankenstein monster had not been mistreated by others, what good qualities would he have shown? In addition to the horror film, learn more about other film genres such as westerns, comedies, thrillers and science fiction films. Make a list of stereotypes you may find in various types of stories and scenes. Include the character's dress and speech. Suppose you were interested in Agatha Christie's Hercule Poirot as a larger-than-life hero: what could be done in the way of exaggerating his physical and mental characteristics? Plan a new set of adventures, using a United States setting, rather than an English one.

National Wildlife Week. Send for pamphlets and folders relating to wildlife. Make posters and puppets of such wildlife creatures as deer, bears and raccoons. Use posters to emphasize endangered wildlife species. Imagine ways to save these creatures and include your ideas in stories, poems and dramatizations. Pretend to have conversations with various animals. For example, you may be a reporter doing a feature TV, newspaper or magazine story and you wish to get a "Save the Animals" message across to the public. Visit each animal in its natural habitat, for example, use background scenery you have painted and puppets you have made.

Youth Art Month. Explore different kinds of visual arts such as animation, free-form sculpture, weaving and design on cloth. Find out how artists like Miro, van Gogh, Picasso and others portrayed subjects like animals or flowers in their drawings and paintings. Choose a theme such as the city or town in which you live, and portray it in as many artistic forms as you can, including: colors, shapes, collages, cardboard sculptures, paper, papier mâché, newspaper cutouts, cloth designs and pictures for belts, bags, tablecloths, novelty towels and so on. Use watercolors, crayon resist, pen and ink, and clay to illustrate different aspects of the city or town. In addition to buildings, try focusing on people's activities in various seasons of the year such as in gardens, landmarks and train stations. Also, portray the local community map, a frisbee contest and so on.

Experiment with various kite designs and display them in the classroom.

Think of representative crafts and/or products your state is known for and make designs for use on or with these items. Display these things on the bulletin board under the caption, "Made in _____ (your state)."

Cut apart cardboard rolls from aluminum foil, wax paper, or toilet paper and use them as foundations for novelty display cups. To make them, make sure your cardboard roll is about three or four inches high: trim off the excess amount. With pencil or pen, mark off eyes, nose, mouth and lines for hair, beards or mustaches as shown in Figure 5-9.

A

B

USE WADS OF CRUSHED NEWSPAPER FOR NOSES, ETC, AND TAPE DIRECTLY ON TUBE.

C

BUILD UP FEATURES WITH WET NEWSPAPER STRIPS DIPPED IN PASTE.

D

ALLOW "CUP" TO DRY AND PAINT ON FEATURES. ACRYLIC PAINTS ARE ESPECIALLY GOOD FOR THIS TYPE OF WORK.

E

IF YOU WISH, CUT A SEPARATE CARDBOARD "EAR" AND ATTACH IT TO THE SIDE OF YOUR CUP.

Figure 5-9

Save Your Vision Week. Create a dialogue between a doctor and his patient about the importance of taking care of the eyes and eyesight. Find out what the inside of an eye looks like and draw it. Advertise this week with posters, make-believe "ads," dramatizations and stories. Investigate careers related to good vision. Make a booklet about eyes, reading habits, why glasses are sometimes necessary, why an "eye" chart is used, etc.

St. Patrick's Day. Find and read a bit of Irish folklore. Some of these stories have material for dramatizations and booklets about related events in nature. Create a picture using different shades of green with paints, construction paper, scrap fabric such as velvet or terry cloth, crayons or a combination of these. Make a pin to wear for this special day—a fairy, leprechaun or shamrock. Learn more about the four-leaf clover and why it is considered a good luck charm. What are other good luck charms you have heard about? Tell some of the stories you have heard about them.

Month: April

Special days and holidays: April Fool's Day (April 1); Booker T. Washington's Birthday; National Library Week; Bike Safety Week; National Arbor Day; Easter; Passover; Pan American Day (April 14).

April Fool's Day. Try to imagine what the first trick or joke in the world might have been and write about it, making up a legend, saga, poem or story. Find out about great comedians of the past, such as Laurel and Hardy, Emmett the Clown, or The Three Stooges. What made them so funny or amusing? Using cardboard, make a funny sign. Or add an original line to the end of a short poem or jingle. Make a collection of other funny or clever jingles. If possible, find and read about the Burma Shave signs, and try the same idea with a favorite product, book or food. Fold a strip of paper accordion-style and take turns filling in the head, body and legs of a funny clown. In your opinion, what makes a joke funny? Make up a story about the first April Fool's Day. Collect cartoons that you think are especially funny. Find out what a cartoonist does, and learn about other related careers.

National Library Week (April 2–8). Find out other duties librarians perform in *your* community and learn more about other careers in this field. Make a floor plan of your community or school library, locating science and story books, the encyclopedia, reference books and the librarian's desk. Make your very own "Quiet!" sign for use when you do your homework or any other activity requiring a lot of concentration. Find your library on a map. How close is it to your house, your school? Make a chart illustrating every "safe" place where you can keep your library card. Or, make a poster on how a book is made. Find out what editors, writers and artists do. Make a bulletin board display and booklets about these careers. This week, pick out a type of book you have not tried reading before—a biography, autobiography, history or travel book—and find a way to describe it.

Bike Safety Week (April 16–27). Make a set of posters showing bike riders observing the rules of the road. Compare these rules to those used by motorcyclists and mopeds riders. Design safety signs especially for bike riders and make a list of where these signs *could* be placed.

National Arbor Day. Find pictures and learn the names of trees found in your region. What others can you recognize immediately besides giant redwoods, for example? What does Smokey the Bear mean when he says, "Only *you* can prevent forest fires"? Learn about conservation-related careers, such as park rangers. Make various leaf shapes out of cardboard, cut them out, place them under a sheet of paper, and rub a crayon over this paper to get a design. Make a leaf lapel pin to wear. Make leaf prints, leaf people, and leaf posters. Think of other types of slogans urging people to help save our trees. Or, do this by telling a story about what will happen when all the trees have been chopped down. A good title might be, "Where Have All the Trees Gone?" In addition to words, use lines, pictures, cartoons and colors to show moods, etc. Make up a new story about Johnny Appleseed, and read Whitman's poem about a tree.

Easter and *Passover,* April's major holidays, are celebrated with a variety of related activities. In addition to those, try enhancing these special days with various "spring" ideas.

Using plasticine, model a "spring thing." Begin with a basic oval or egg-shape. Then use this shape to make an imaginary spring animal or another creature. If you like, make a model of Humpty Dumpty.

Make a catalogue of spring flowers and plants. Discover and learn the original Latin names of these plants. See "National Arbor Day" activities, most of which can be used in a spring theme.

Learn about festivals in foreign countries that are related to spring. In books about customs, you are likely to find that most of these festivals are very old. Find and dramatize some of the stories associated with these spring festivals.

Month: May

Special days and holidays: May Day/Law Day (May 1); Jumping Frog Contest in California; Mother's Day; Kite Festival in Japan (May 5); Armed Forces Day; Memorial Day.

Activities:

May Day/Law Day. Read how and find out why the ancient Romans and Druids celebrated May Day. May Day was also celebrated during the Middle Ages; English villages competed in a contest to see which one had the tallest Maypole. Find out what those maypoles looked like and design your own. Make May baskets and diorama scenes of early celebrations, decorate your room with crepe paper versions of Lily-of-the-Valley and daisies. Find out how May Day is celebrated in Ireland, Greece, Italy and some of our own colleges. Use this information to make bulletin board displays and booklets.

May Day is also celebrated as Law Day. Find out what lawyers and legal secretaries do. Can you think of stereotypes related to these careers? For example, does a legal secretary really have a glamorous exciting week all of the time? Pick out an important legal matter, such as one relating to pollution and the environment, pose a question and take a stand, either "for" or "against." Then use this information to make a case in a debate or make-believe trial. Who are the parties involved? Who are the defendants, plaintiffs and witnesses?

Mother's Day. Give a different look to Mother's Day this year by making different types of cards for a change. For example, fold a piece of pastel-colored construction paper in half and cut out a silhouette of mother. Decorate it with spring flowers and write a message inside as shown in Figure 5-10.

Figure 5-10

Or, cut out a large piece of construction or wallpaper to look like mother's apron. Measure contrasting pocket pieces of another colored paper and staple these to the lower half of the apron, making it resemble pockets. Place a written message, drawing or small gift inside each pocket and give the card to Mother. (See Figure 5-11.)

Figure 5-11

Use Whistler's famous painting as an inspiration for your own picture or story. Make a Mother's Day book with nine pages, filling each page with a message for mother on her day and/or pictures that begin with the following letters: M-O-T-H-E-R or H-A-P-P-Y M-O-T-H-E-R-S D-A-Y or H-I M-O-M. Make up a song for Mother's Day. What other symbols can you think of that could be used for Mother's Day?

Kite Festival (May 5). Although this special day is celebrated in Japan, it can be used as a source of ideas and fun. For example, make and decorate kites out of cardboard, cartons, paper, cellophane, newspaper, construction paper or cloth. Find out what conditions are needed in order for kites to fly. Think of other objects that "fly," such as blimps, balloons, airplanes and gliders, and read about the scientific principles involved. Make models of each craft, and include them in a special classroom display. Relate the work of da Vinci, the Wright Brothers and Lindbergh. Look at pictures of Japanese kites.

Armed Forces Day. Learn about different careers in the armed services—what kinds of skills do sailors, soldiers, marines and air force people learn? Who are some famous sailors and soldiers in history? Make figures of them in cardboard, paper or pipe cleaners and dress them in the service uniform of your choice. Make "settings" for these figures from cardboard cartons. Find out the motto of each division of the armed services: what does it mean? How does your state celebrate Armed Forces Day?

Memorial Day. Using the colors red, white and blue, make designs with colored pencils, paints, ribbon or wool. Collect pictures from magazines and newspapers showing how Memorial Day is observed in various parts of the country and display them on the bulletin board. Think of as many of your own ways as possible to observe this day.

Month: June

Special days and holidays: Flag Day; Father's Day; Children's Day; Summer, June 21; first "flying saucers" reported on June 24, 1947.

Activities:

Flag Day. Find pictures of earlier U.S. flags and try to draw some of them. Put them and their stories on a bulletin board display. Put on a play about the legend of Betsy Ross. Write a different legend which tells the story of one of the earlier versions of our flag. Look in a dictionary or thesaurus for other words that may mean the same thing as the word "flag." Make a chart showing the correct way to display our flag and give a demonstration of some of them. Describe these ways in your own words.

Children's Day. Read and illustrate poems about children using Milne's book, *When We Were Six* as a source. Learn about a babysitter's responsibilities, particularly during emergencies.

How does a babysitter amuse a restless child or take care of a tired, angry or frightened child? Make figures of children working and playing; and also make figures of children in the foreign lands of your choice.

Father's Day. Make a list of items that symbolize Father's Day and use one or more of them to make a card for your father. Then make a list of all the words that describe your father and use them in your greeting-card message, or include them in a "hidden word" puzzle. Instead of a card, draw a picture of dad at his favorite pastime using the title, "Dad, You're the Greatest." Make a puzzle from it. What do words like "forefather," "city fathers," "grandfather" and "fatherland" mean? Learn other ways to say father in a foreign language, and compare these words. Find examples of these words in our own language, such as "paternal." Read and dramatize the story of *William Tell*. Imagine yourself in young Tell's place: what would you have done: What might have happened?

Summer, June 21. Make a list of summer recreations and sports. Illustrate them using pictures, photographs, or dioramas, and make a bulletin board or a series of dioramas entitled, "Those Lazy Days of Summer." You may also wish to include some of your state's summer attractions and design a poster for some of them. Think of different ways to keep cool besides turning on the air conditioner—and save energy at the same time—and include them in a booklet. Decide what colors are "cool," find matching pieces of construction paper, cut these pieces in various shapes and arrange them in an attractive summer design. Or, use pictures from a magazine instead. Make a set of postcards showing pictures of good places to visit nearby, and write messages on the back of them. Or include them in a bulletin board display entitled, "Wish You Were Here." Make up cartoons or a series of them about summer, entitled "Still Under the Weather." Learn about different types of seashells and fish. Make shell designs for drawings, paintings, pins, and cushions. Make a larger-than-life set of figures and include them on a beach scene where they can be arranged in from time to time. Use their poses as the basis of line drawings.

Children's Books About the Holidays

Arthur, Mildred H., *Holidays and Legend*, Harvey House, New York, 1971.

Barth, Edna, *Turkeys, Pilgrims and Indian Corn*, The Seabury Press, New York, 1975.

Witches, Pumpkins, and Grinning Ghosts, and *Lilies, Rabbits and Painted Eggs.* The Seabury Press, New York, 1975.

Childcraft, *The How and Why Library: Holidays and Customs*, Volume 9, Field Enterprises Educational Corp., Chicago, 1973.

Churchill, Richard E., *Holiday Hullabaloo,* Franklin Watts: New York, 1977.

Ickis, Marguerite, *The Book of Festival Holidays,* Dodd, Mead, & Co., New York, 1964.

Johnson, Lois, *Happy New Year Round the World,* Rand McNally, New York, 1966.

Myers, Robert, *Celebrations: The Complete Book of American Holidays,* Doubleday & Co., Garden City, New York, 1972.

Sechrist, Elizabeth Hough, *Red Letter Days: A Book of Holiday Customs,* Macrae Smith Co., New York, 1965.

D. HINTS FOR ALL HOLIDAYS

1. Whenever possible, try incorporating tales and customs from other lands into various reading and language arts activities.

2. Use "chalk talk" or pre-cut figures as a storytelling device.

3. Keep a holiday "goodies" box where children can find something to make or do after completing regular assignments. Hint: include related reading and math activities and games.

4. Provide a "Sharing Period" for pupils to share something they have done or made, if they wish. Give further recognition to their efforts by displaying items in a classroom display entitled, "This Week's Specials."

5. Have a "Holiday Countdown" by planning a special, quiet activity or treat two or three days before the actual holiday. Or, include it in a "Class Events" calendar.

6. Remember that atmosphere counts. Include pictures and other items of the season as well as of the holiday itself.

7. Allow changes in the room to take place gradually.

8 Experiment with exaggerations as one way of avoiding holiday stereotypes. For example, must all holiday bells or candles look alike in shape and color? (If you use a fatter candle, there is the possibility of designing a variety of figures from it by scraping away wax or adding decorations.)

9. Have a definite plan in mind for taking down decorations right before or soon after the holidays, as well as for something the children can look forward to when they return from vacation.

6

INTRODUCING THE COMMUNITY AND ITS HELPERS TO THE COME-ALIVE CLASSROOM

In practically any grade, a community topic may be extended from a familiar to a fascinating theme for children. Its geography, history, arts and other contributions can often be included in several related areas of the curriculum. Also, a community's sources and resources are within easy reach.

USING THE COMMUNITY AS A TEACHING AID

Whether your pupils' community is large or small, it can be used entirely "as is" to make curriculum areas more meaningful to children. These areas and their "starting points" are shown below. Try looking for ways to combine or compare the following direct experiences in:

Language Arts

1. *A Community Alphabet.* Find places, people and community activities whose names begin with each letter in the alphabet.
2. *Community Scrapbook.* Look in the local paper for pictures that can be related to a particular theme, such as

"How We Save Energy" and "Our Community's Heritage."

3. *All About My Street.* Make individual street maps. Write descriptions of buildings on your block such as the library, supermarket, etc. Write about the changes that take place on your block in the morning, at noon and at night, being sure to include such things as the shadiest side, children's activities during a certain season, and so on.

4. *Directions for Playing a Sidewalk Game.* One child may give oral directions on how to play a sidewalk game while his or her classmate tries to follow them. Or pupils may design and write "Games to Play in _____ Season," a booklet.

5. Find out what other languages are spoken in the community and learn a few simple, everyday words in those languages.

6. Take a poll on a particular topic, such as what services people think would be good for the community or whether a certain tree or other landmark should be saved.

7. Plan a short interview to learn about work done in your community. Talk to doctors, lawyers, beauticians, park maintenance persons, artists, etc.

8. Visit an exhibit or festival in your community and write about it as a newspaper reporter might, being sure to include answers to questions asking who, what, where, when and why.

9. Write a letter to the local newspaper editor praising something or somebody, or suggesting areas in which improvements should be made.

10. What is changing in your community? Use next weekend to take a walk and find out. Write or draw a picture about what you have seen and display it on the bulletin board under the caption, "What's New."

11. Make up riddles about your community.

12. Mix and match community words, such as bus, garage, depot, station, train, taxi, airport, school, policeman, truck, house, city hall, park, etc.

The Arts

1. Design a poster advertising an upcoming event in your community or an event that you have made up.
2. Make silhouettes of community landmarks—or places you think should be designated as such. Try experimenting with contrasting shades of paper.
3. Design a postage stamp for your community's tricentennial. How will things have changed?
4. Find articles and/or pictures of local celebrities in the arts—painting, acting, photography, writing, music and dance. Perhaps you could invite one or more of them to speak to the class.
5. Learn a few crafts, songs and dances of ethnic groups in your community.
6. Using the outline of your transit system (bus or train) as a guide, design a similar motif for a tee shirt, tray or poster. Include the names of station stops and the current color code.
7. Think of ways to beautify your community and include them in descriptions, drawings and dioramas.
8. Using a variety of sounds, make up a song or poem about your community. Sing this song or recite this poem with a tape recording of sounds and music as a background.
9. What buildings, monuments or other works of art can your community take pride in? Use this item as a motif for a poster design.
10. Pretend you have a camera and are focusing it on the most scenic or colorful areas of your community. Describe this scene in words and finally in pictures. Find examples of beautiful (local) trees and flowers, too.

11. Get involved with "brick art." Make a design or draw a picture using various lengths and widths of brick shapes. Make a sculpture using "cardboard box" bricks. Paint these bricks different colors and arrange them to make a design. Make miniature cardboard brick shapes and arrange them in various geometrical designs.

12. Make pictures of your community using sets of contrasting colors, such as black and white, orange and brown, dark blue and light blue, purple and beige, black and grey. You may also wish to describe your feelings as you use these combinations.

13. Design a modern sculpture for a spot in your community—in the park, for the lawn in front of your house or other building, or your yard or garden. What other features does this sculpture have? How can you make it "fit" its setting? What materials would you use to help do this?

14. Experiment with shadows on a sunny day. What kinds of interesting ones can you make on the sidewalk? Against a building?

15. Make a plant art motif or sculpture or picture, using a variety of materials such as crepe paper and wire, string, newspaper, cellophane tape and sponges to form whole or different parts of plants.

Social Studies

1. Find out how people communicate in your town, using signals, hand motions, etc. What people use these kinds of motions in their jobs? What do these signals mean?

2. What are some of the ways you can make your town a better place to live? What kinds of help can local town agencies give you?

3. Suppose you tried to trace your community's roots? Where would you look for information?

4. Make a list of all the various jobs and professions found in your community. To make the task easier, use broad categories such as "Medical Professions," "Recreation," "Environment," "Transportation," etc. Then list types of jobs under each of these categories.

5. What are some ethnic holidays and festivals celebrated in your community?

6. If possible, make models of places of interest for tourists to visit in your community, using cardboard, cartons, papier mâché or any combination of these.

7. Portray outstanding historical events of your town by way of tableaus or dioramas.

8. Compare another community with your own, finding differences and similarities in distance, size, climate, places of interest, and so on.

9. How does your community celebrate such holidays as the Fourth of July? Labor Day? Memorial Day?

10. Make a map of your community in any of the following ways:

    a. A large mural-sized map, showing names of streets, symbols for places of interest, highways, main roads, railroad stations, schools, parks, etc.

    b. A three-dimensional map. First sketch blocks and streets lightly in pencil on a piece of cardboard. Then gradually build up buildings, hills, etc. with clay or papier mâché and small cardboard boxes.

    c. Make a larger map by using different sizes of boxes representing "blocks." Paint on symbols for stores, schools, highways, and other places.

11. If possible, try to see how your community has changed by examining earlier maps. How did streets and street names change? What buildings were standing then?

12. Find poems that seem appropriate to your town or city. Copy one or two of the best ones, place them in the center of the bulletin board and make suitable illustrations to use as a "frame."

13. What do the signs in your community say? Collect as many different messages as you can. Would you ever improve such messages by adding pictures? Or explaining with words alone?

14. What kinds of impressions would a visitor from earlier historical periods have of modern day life in your town? How would he or she feel about seeing new inventions and conveniences? Do you think he or she would be frightened by these things?

15. Find out what groups of people first lived in your town. How did their lifestyles differ? What contributions did they make? What hardships did they face?

16. Take a survey of the different types of homes in your community. In what ways are these homes different? Make up your own "gallery of homes." What kinds of things must you know about buying a home?

17. Pretend you are a person living in your community one hundred years ago, choose some things that matter the most to you, and write about them from your viewpoint. Or write an imaginary dialogue between you and a citizen of the future.

Science

1. What kinds of birds, trees and flowers can be found in your town? Make a graph of them, including their names and the times of the year in which they can be seen.

2. Make a set of fossils or prints of things that are found in your community, such as leaves, animal footprints, and the like.

3. Try graphing rainy days in your city or town. What week did it rain the most? In that week was the sun out nearly every day? Which month was the rainiest? The sunniest?

4. Try to obtain an areial picture (photograph) of your local area. What do you notice about its shape and size? Then do a related experiment. Choose an object or person to "focus" on (a car or house) about one-half block

away. What happened? Now walk closer to that item and see what happens. Draw pictures showing before and after views.

5. *Community reflections.* Suppose you wanted to see if your hair looked neat. You are also outside and do not happen to have a mirror with you. Name the places or things you would use to see your reflection—besides glass in store windows and doors.

6. Find out what science-related exhibits are available in your local museum and write a newspaper report about them.

Math

1. Take some time out to investigate community and state space. First draw an outline of your state and mark the location of your city or town inside, as in Figure 6-1. What cities or towns are you the closest to, the furthest from? Figure out the approximate distance. What is the position of your city or town on this map—northeast, west, southeast, north?

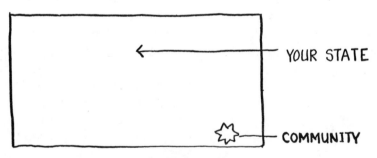

Figure 6-1

2. Try pricing a particular item in two different stores. Is the price about the same, lower or higher?

3. Make graphs comparing certain types of things, such as types of pets owned by the neighbors on your block and nearby area.

4. During your next walk, make a collection of shapes found in your community. For example, the outline of a

"No Parking" sign looks like a rectangle. Look at outlines of store signs, baby carriages, bicycles, canes, umbrellas, cars, etc. Draw their outlines on a sheet of paper. Then separate these outlines into various categories, such as "circles," "squares," "a combination of shapes." What kinds of shapes seem to be found in most places?

5. Keep a record of your local team's scores and average these scores out at the end of the season.

EXPLORING DIFFERENT CAREERS WITH CHILDREN

In a short time, children become acquainted with traditional community helpers, such as policemen, firemen, teachers and doctors—and learn about these different careers as well. For many pupils, this is a step in the right direction, because they may also hear about related positions in law, health care and education. Too, you have a foundation from which to branch to other professions and vocations, and a way of widening the range, rather than influencing any particular choices.

One way of exploring other careers is by beginning with jobs in the community itself listed in the Yellow Pages. Have children look through this section to see what other workers do for a living. Your pupils will also find names of related positions, such as medical technician or electrician in other sources like the newspaper.

Perhaps your class can find more examples of these fields, as well as vocations that at least sound interesting. In addition to the local phone book, try the classified section in your town's newspaper. What other kinds of positions are advertised? What do some abbreviations mean? What kinds of skills are probably necessary or good to have? Can pupils think of how their school work can be related to these skills? Make a list of promising or otherwise appealing career choices. Look in the library for books about careers. If possible, arrange for one or more professional people to visit your class and talk about their work.

Still another way involves considering opportunities available in subject areas such as ecology and mathematics. Include this information on a bulletin board or learning center display and encourage pupils' contributions.

To make lists of career choices manageable, use larger categories. For example, under transportation careers, include such jobs as bus drivers, truck drivers, train conductors, dispatchers, and so on. Workers like station managers, weather specialists, track inspectors, and others might also be placed in specific types of transportation—rail, air and land. Certainly, all of these positions require good reading, math and management skills. If pupils investigate these and other careers further, they will also find that people in any community need and rely on each other in many different ways.

In addition to these suggestions for exploring careers, try any or all of the activities below:

1. *Language Experiences.* Children may even be helping some community workers on a part time basis. How do they like these jobs? What kinds of skills are they using right now? What kind of training was necessary?

2. *A Day in the Life.* From books and people who are actually working in a given field, find out what a typical work week is like. Use this information on charts to be included in a learning center about a given field.

3. Keep a file of interesting careers in the classroom library.

4. Simplify and use situations in a few appealing careers. Learn the words of a career's particular lingo and what they mean. Write them on separate 3 × 5-inch cards and put them in alphabetical order. Or place these word cards in two columns and match words with similar meanings in one column to their "partners" in the second. Try to find examples of math problems involved and adapt them for classroom use. Do science experiments that can be related in some way to a given career.

5. *Bigger Than Life.* Find out what's true about a certain field in several sources, rather than trying to understand this field from the same viewpoint. For example, what are some of the hidden benefits and drawbacks of this job. What are other things that make this job more interesting than it sounds?

6. *Career Classifying.* Investigate other sources to find out about some lesser-known, but related careers in a certain field. Then list them on separate cards to be included in a file in the classroom library.

7. *Courtesy Pays.* Many times, people must hurry to and from work, and must get from one place to another in very crowded conditions. Think of as many ways as you can to "make time" in traveling under these conditions, and illustrate these ways with pictures, filmstrips or words. Remember that the medium is the message! Use your imagination!

8. *Career Capers.* After learning more about a particular career, list every word that would describe it in some way. Then have one or more of your classmates see this list and try to guess what career you are describing. How close have their guesses come?

9. *Who Are You?* Take turns in acting out one part of a job of your choice.

10. *Up the Career Ladder.* For a career that interests you, find out what early experiences could be applied to that position. Then imagine and write a make-believe resumé or letter of application for that job.

11. *Career Booklets.* Make and label scrapbooks for various careers. In addition to written descriptions, try including pictures from magazines and newspapers that might be related to that career.

12. *Fitting the Picture.* This time, write down *your* idea of the perfect banker, doctor, crossing guard, etc. Learn how your expectations match up with the facts about the job you are interested in.

13. *I've Been Working on My Favorite Career.* Using the information you have about a particular career, write a song about it to the tune of "I've Been Working on the Railroad." Make this song as humorous or as serious as you wish.

14. *Putting It All Together.* Draw or cut a picture from a magazine depicting a person working at some kind of

job. Paste it on a piece of cardboard of the same size. After allowing it to dry, cut it in jigsaw puzzle pieces. Mix up these pieces and challenge one of your classmates to build the puzzle.

15. *Stay Tuned.* Become an authority about any given field of your choice. Then do any or all of the following: allow interested classmates to interview you; set up a related display or bulletin board; make a booklet or scrapbook about the career; or write a one-act play involving two or more classmates or puppets.

16. *Career Crossword.* First, write down all the words that could be related in some way to a career of your choice. Then design a simple or more complicated crossword puzzle about it and challenge your classmates to solve it.

17. *Hand in Hand.* Try thinking ahead for this one. Pretend that you were not able to work in the career of your choice for some reason. What alternatives would be just as appealing? To find them, write three or four of your interests or abilities on a sheet of paper. Then list possible alternative job choices under as many of these as you can. After listing these in order of preference, investigate one or more jobs that would interest you.

18. *Career Preview.* Make a figure of a worker in one of your career choices. Using cloth scraps, crepe or construction paper, dress him (or her) accordingly. Then do any or all of the following: (1) Write a brief description, such as "I am an ambulance attendant. I help the people of my community by _____, _____, and _____."; or (2) Make a cardboard background for your worker to stand against. Include models of the trappings of his (or her) trade or profession, and display this item for the class to see.

19. *Career Profiles.* Make up one or more riddles describing a particular career. How many people guessed correctly?

20. *Facts and Forecasts.* Look in sources such as almanacs and news and business journals/magazines for infor-

mation about the groups of people in certain fields. Learn to read simpler graphs or make up your own graphs showing some aspect of these positions. What kinds of predictions are being made for the types of jobs available in the future? Do any of these jobs appeal to you?

PROJECTS TO GIVE A SENSE OF COMMUNITY

Often, children who are challenged to use their own community as a starting point for learning experiences manage to accomplish useful things on their own. Try motivating them with any or all of the following suggestions.

1. *Invent an anti-litter device.* Littering is a form of pollution, yet people often forget to pick up their empty bottles and bags. Try inventing a device or other contraption to absorb this litter and/or remind people to clean up. Experiment with different materials, particularly those that can withstand much wear and tear.

2. *Project your community of the future.* Decide what may have changed in the next decade and how these changes will affect your community. Perhaps you can write a scenario using Toffler's *Future Shock* as a starting point. In what ways might members of your town or city be caught by future shock?

3. *Community Diary.* Whether you are on your way to school, the store, a friend's house, or work, try to notice what changes have taken place in your area during the last week or so. Describe them from your point of view, telling whether you think such changes would benefit your community.

4. *It Pays to Advertise.* Make posters advertising your community of the future and any of its upcoming attractions.

5. *Visitor's Guide.* This can be in the form of a large map of your town with cut-out pictures of places of interest. Or separate folders, tour guides and pamphlets.

6. *Community Scrapbook*. Make a scrapbook of the events of the current year, such as pictures and accounts of that record snow or rainfall, the day your school won an important game or that coveted championship or had an important visitor speak to pupils.

7. *Classroom Contributors*. If you hold a job, such as delivering newspapers, have helped someone in some way, or have done something outstanding for your school or community, you deserve recognition! Perhaps an accompanying "profile" of the outstanding pupil of the week or month can be included in a special display in the classroom.

8. *Commemorate an important date in your community's history or recent achievement*. Make up "You Were There" scripts, pictures, murals and puppets. Write to your local chamber of commerce for information, and check other sources at the library.

9. *Call citizens' attention to a clean, healthy environment*. Using pictures you have drawn, show what happens before something is done to improve a given spot in your community. Explain what *you* think was possible to keep an attractive spot looking as it now does. Include the "rewards" of keeping an area neat. Make a class display of posters showing these and other aspects of a clean, healthy local environment. Then invite parents to see them as well as attend a program given by the class.

10. *Help a worthy organization, such as the SPCA* by volunteering some of your free time helping out with odd jobs.

WHAT OTHER COMMUNITY HELPERS DO

Next to their parents' occupations, children are most likely to hear about traditional community helpers—policemen, firemen, teachers, store clerks, etc. They will also have at least read about administrative positions, environmental jobs and others; for careers like these also benefit the community. By directing children's attention to these and other lesser-known occupations, you will be expanding pupils' horizons—and giving ideas of satisfying careers. For example, the following workers serve the community as:

real estate agents	business managers
teacher aides	typists
librarians	artists
mechanics	secretaries
newspaper editors	veterinarians
computer operators and programmers	health care workers, such as medical technicians
salesmen, saleswomen	truck drivers
writers	gasoline station owners
day care teachers	telephone operators and installers
building inspectors	
construction workers	plumbers
engineers	locksmiths
school administrators	news agents
travel agents	news reporters
tax collectors	meteorologists
water and gas meter readers	waitresses

To explore these and other workers' occupations more thoroughly, try using suggestions given in the previous section, "Exploring Other Careers with Children." In addition to these ideas, you may also wish to provide various used articles of clothing for pupils to use in role playing, or explore how the workers listed above use basic reading and math skills, as well as an ability to relate well with others.

7

HOW TO MAKE HISTORY AND GEOGRAPHY COME ALIVE

Using a different focus, you can make learning experiences in history and geography take on much meaning for pupils. History, for example, is more than facts when children work with sagas. True, sagas are fictionalized accounts of one or more family generations. But they also involve historical settings and geography. At the same time, geography influences peoples' ideas about their surroundings, near and far, and these ideas are often expressed as folk tales, or stories. Such stories can be used to enrich children's studies of geography. This chapter includes ideas for using these sources as well as ways to make social studies an enlightening experience for children.

MAKING AND USING INDIVIDUAL SOCIAL STUDIES KITS

Besides reinforcing important concepts and motivating children, social studies kits will save you much time in the long run, for everything needed by an individual or a small group is placed in one container. Little time is lost in finding items such as pencils, clay or construction paper. Moreover, these kits may be large enough to hold one or more completed products, or at least hold separate envelopes for children's written work. You will also find that such papers are easier to correct and/or evaluate.

In making social studies kits, you may decide to use one of the following types:

1. *Map kits.* Among the many possible materials in these kits, pencils, maps, construction paper and rulers are

often included. Or you may decide to have children make a certain kind of map, such as one made of papier mâché, paper or clay. Compasses, both real or models, may be included.

2. *Geography kits.* You have a wide range to choose from here. Usually, the most effective kits tend to emphasize a single aspect of a country (U.S. or other land) or state. A helpful addition to this type of kit is a small map of the country or state pasted inside. Word and picture cards may also be included.

3. *History kits.* Take your cue from suggestions given above. In addition to various reading and research activities, you may also wish to include a related learning experience in the arts or a game. The main emphasis should be on the concepts and skills you are trying to have children learn.

4. *Miscellaneous categories kits,* such ast those about "Cities," "Indians," "Explorers," and so on.

5. *Social studies kits for slower and/or more advanced students.* For example, pupils who experience reading or other difficulties may benefit more from a kit that uses many pictures as substitutes for the printed word. Materials for these pupils are likely to include shorter items, games and activities. On the other hand, advanced pupils may benefit from more difficult and detailed activity cards and equipment, or reading material that provides additional insights and challenges.

6. *Unusual social studies kits.* If your class is learning about families, you may just consider having one or more kits resemble miniature doll houses and accompanying activity cards. Shoe boxes make ideal containers for such kits, although other smaller cartons allow for greater variety and may be a bit stronger. Use papier mâché for furniture. (See Figure 7-1.)

Beds, stoves, sofas, and tables are made of small boxes, or cardboard strip foundations and covered with papier-mâché strips.

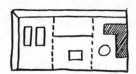

A INSIDE OF SHOE BOX — DRAW OR MARK LOCATIONS OF ROOMS AND FURNITURE.

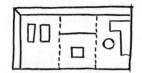

B CUT AND TAPE SMALL BOXES OR CARDBOARD PIECES AS FOUNDATIONS FOR FURNITURE. ALL OF THESE PIECES SHOULD BE SMALL. USING WET NEWSPAPER STRIPS (WITH PASTE), BUILD UP THESE FOUNDATIONS INTO FURNITURE.

MAKING A CHAIR

C CUT A STRIP OF CARDBOARD, ROLL IT INTO A CIRCLE, AND TAPE IT TO THE FLOOR OF THE BOX. PLACE A BIT OF CRUSHED NEWSPAPER INSIDE FOR SEAT, AS SHOWN.

D CRISSCROSS PASTED NEWSPAPER STRIPS ALL AROUND, FORMING THE CHAIR AS YOU WORK.

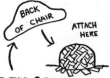

E CUT THIS PATTERN FROM A PIECE OF CARDBOARD. PLACE IT IN BACK OF THE CHAIR, AND COVER IT WITH PASTED PAPER STRIPS.

F PAINT THE COMPLETED CHAIR OR DECORATE IT BY PASTING ON SUITABLE CLOTH SCRAPS. ALLOW DRYING TIME.

G TAPE CARDBOARD STRIPS TO FLOOR. STUFF WITH COTTON, FABRIC SCRAPS, OR NEWSPAPER AND BUILD UP WITH PAPIER MÂCHÉ STRIPS.

H COMPLETED BED

Figure 7-1

Social studies kits also will vary in content, size and even shape. For example, there are many types of containers to choose from to put it all together, such as:

Boxes from shirts, boots, shoes, oatmeal and cereal.

Tins from fruitcake, candy and cookies.

Bags, both plastic and cloth.

Plastic pails, plastic containers.

Other Important Materials

In nearly all kits, you should include the following items:

- *Code* with colors, symbols, etc. For example, to distinguish geography kits from history kits, use certain colors or the same size boxes for you and your pupils to locate easily. Gummed labels or bits of adhesive tape make instant "markers" or codes.

- *Direction sheet* or activity card should be taped inside each kit. For kits with many smaller items, try including a checklist. If the kit contains something for children to make, paste a picture of how this completed item may look.

Handy Items

(List of everything included in the kit.)

3 × 5-inch cards	Rulers
puzzles	Construction paper
pictures, folders from tourist offices	Clay (in sandwich bag)
	String, yarn
Paper	Maps
Pencils	Clothespins
Scissors	Small figures

While these social studies kits can be used to enrich units and lessons, their other possibilities include:

- use as homework assignments.
- lesson supplements.

- individual, long-term projects for one child or a small group.
- a series of kits may be developed from a single kit.

NINE WAYS TO ENHANCE A HISTORICAL THEME

Many times, you can give a new look to a familiar theme by exploring it from a different viewpoint or by using a new source altogether. The suggestions below include specific ways to do this.

1. *Pictures (or photographs) of old movie stills* are fun to look at and often provide hints as to the types of clothing worn, popular activities, cars (if any) and customs. You might ask older pupils to examine copies of old newspapers on microfilm at the library. Advertisements, pictures of fashions, reviews of books and movies help to give a broader perspective and a better feeling of a given historical period.

2. *Views of tomorrow.* In nearly every historical period, people were thinking about or preparing for the future, directly and indirectly. Although they were interested in improving their own lives, these earlier generations helped people in future times. Have children find examples of such thinking. Later on, find biographies and autobiographies of men and women who seemed to be thinking ahead of their time. Use this information in dioramas, displays, bulletin boards, booklets, paintings and models. Finally, all of this information may be a good introduction to the future of children.

3. *Novels based on the same historical period.* Besides enjoying the story, children may dramatize outstanding scenes, find unusual words or expressions to look up, and feel inspired to write their own original stories, plays and poems.

4. *Miniature museum.* Using cardboard, clay, or papier mâché, make models of various items people might have

used in a given period. Label these items, and be sure to include a small card describing how and where the artifact was "found" (pupils can make up a plausible location) and how it was used.

5. *Unsung heroes and heroines.* Pupils draw up a list of historical personalities who deserve more recognition than they may have received, or were even omitted altogether. Later on, children may choose sides in explaining why or why not that particular person should be recognized. A survey might also yield some surprising results.

6. *The ways things might have been if . . .* Have children imagine what would have happened if a certain historical event was changed for one or more reasons. Try to imagine the consequences that followed.

7. *Room frieze.* On a strip of wrapping paper about 24 inches wide and a few feet long (use classroom measurements to determine size more accurately), draw symbols and figures representing main events of the historical period being studied. Then display your frieze along one or more classroom walls.

8. *Fact or fiction.* Find examples of actual and possible stereotypes and replace them with what is known to be true. For example, the so-called "Dark Ages" is a misnomer. Not all Indians wore feather headdresses and lived in teepees. Compare facts to fiction by making a filmstrip, flyer, cartoon, booklet or by drawing pictures.

9. *Emphasize social history.* As you know, history is more than certain changes and events of the past, leaders and dates. Help pupils get a better perspective by learning how ordinary people of a given time worked and played. What kinds of jobs did these people have, schools did they have, games did they play? All kinds of understandings and activities can be developed from this area alone. Specific ideas are given in the example in the next section.

ONE WAY TO EXPLORE SOCIAL HISTORY:
HOW COLONIAL CHILDREN WORKED AND PLAYED

In addition to concepts and chronicles of famous events and people, the activities of ordinary people—how they dressed, traveled, worked and played—should be considered. These features help make history less remote to many children, and act as sources for further reading, research and art projects.

To find out more about the social history of a given period, check museums and children's books in particular. Then look, read and take some notes. Organize your information by including one category apiece per sheet of paper, such as "Recreation," "Crafts," "Types of Work," "Transportation," "Homes," "Child Life" and "Education."

Under each category, list only that information which can be adapted to further class activities and bulletin boards. Whenever possible, make rough sketches of people at work and play. You will probably think of other ideas once you begin. If your pupils happen to be learning about the colonies, for example, you will find the following activities useful:

1. Make up different versions of games that colonial children played, such as marbles, tag, hopscotch, etc. Think of different "winning" strategies and describe them.

2. Find out about the different lifestyles of children living in northern and southern colonies—houses they lived in, foods they ate, toys and pets they had and how they dressed.

3. Pick out a year during the colonial period and find out what famous people you would have heard about, and perhaps even spoken to, if you were a child living in those times. What kinds of things would you be learning? What household chores would you have done?

4. Use what you are learning in arithmetic as an idea or "starting point" for a rhyme.

5. Write a journal of a colonial school child's life during a typical week. Is this child living in a town or a rural area? Describe it.

6. Play "Categories." On separate 3 × 5-inch cards, write a single present day or colonial chore. Mix these cards up and place them face down. Toss two die to find out the number of cards you may pick up at one time. Separate the cards in your hand according to present-day and colonial chores. The player having the most cards containing colonial chores is the winner. Of course, another child may be selected to act as an impartial judge. Play other versions of this game, or expand it to include different categories pertaining to colonial life.

7. Read about the childhood of a well-known colonial man or woman. Would you have chosen this person as a hero or heroine had you been a child living in those times. Use your imagination in telling *your* version of the story.

8. Pretend that you are a child living in colonial times. You awake early one morning. Tell what you would probably see as you looked outside your door or window. What kind of day is it? Did you see any animals or people? Are any other members of your family awake yet? If so, who?

9. Make a simple hornbook from cardboard and paste a copy of one or more of your lessons on it. (See Figure 7-2.)

10. The following books were popular with colonial children: *Robinson Crusoe*, *Gulliver's Travels*, and *Mother Goose*. Read and dramatize an especially interesting scene from all or one of these.

11. Make a toy using only twigs, leaves and paper. Write a description of it on a separate card, telling how it is used or played.

12. Make a list of all of the different foods you would eat, clothes you would wear, pets you might have, chores you would do, subjects you would study, and skills

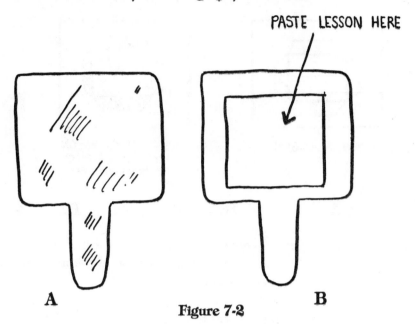

PASTE LESSON HERE

A   B

Figure 7-2

your parents would probably teach you if you lived as a child during colonial times. Try not to include similar "modern" activities, such as running errands or caring for a younger brother or sister.

13. Find a convenience colonists had to live without and try to imagine yourself getting along without it. Name some things that would be *easy* to live without and some that would be *difficult* to live without.

14. Draw a portrait of a quilt design. First cut colored paper and/or scraps of fabrics to fit the design you have drawn. Then sew or glue pieces in appropriate places. You may expand this in a quilt. You can also use this activity to explore other geometric shapes—and use them in designs. (Figure 7-3.)

15. Try to find pictures of your city or town as it might have looked in colonial times—or pick a town that sounds interesting to you.

16. Make up a colonial alphabet. Use each letter of the alphabet in a word that names a toy, activity or item in a

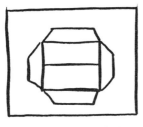

DRAW A DESIGN

PASTE OR SEW ON
APPROPRIATE PIECES OF
CONSTRUCTION PAPER OR
FABRIC.

A   Figure 7-3   **B**

colonial child's environment. For the difficult letters, such as X, substitute a suitable colonial name (as done in hornbooks) as "Xerxes."

17. On white paper, draw a picture of some aspect of a colonial child's life—at home, in school, with friends or with a favorite pet. Cut out all of the figures and other features in your drawing. Then mount your picture on black construction paper. (Figure 7-4.)

CUT ALONG OUTLINES
OF FIGURES IN YOUR
DRAWING.

PLACE YOUR CUT-OUT ON
A BLACK PIECE OF CON-
STRUCTION PAPER.

A   Figure 7-4   **B**

18. Draw a picture of your classroom. Then draw another picture showing the type of schoolroom that might have been used in colonial times. Now place these two pictures side by side. Looking at them, name as many differences between the "old" and the "new" as you can.

19. Make a plaque featuring a colonial child. First draw an outline on cardboard. Crush a few pieces of newspaper and tape them on various parts of the drawn figure, particularly in prominent areas. Complete modeling the figure with papier-mâché strips. Allow it to dry and paint it. (See Figure 7-5.)

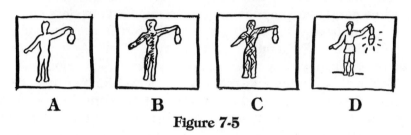

A   B   C   D

Figure 7-5

20. Make models of toys made by and used by colonial children. Examples of such toys include whistles, tops, rocking horses, dolls, and an Ark with its own set of animals.

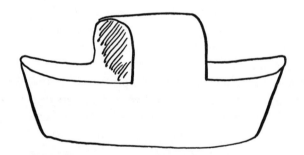

AN OUTLINE OF THE KIND OF "ARK"-TOY COLONIAL CHILDREN MIGHT HAVE USED.

Figure 7-6

INVENTING SAGAS AS A WAY OF UNDERSTANDING HISTORY

One way of having pupils use what they already know in history, including writing and research skills, is by using sagas. In sagas, any variety of historical periods serves as background for stories of fictional individuals or families trying to solve or overcome their problems. At other times, sagas involve a family's or individual's changing lifestyles from one generation to the next in an interesting story. These features make sagas worthwhile reading—and writing.

To make sagas work for your pupils, begin with a background material familiar to the class, such as a history unit or a community history. Sometimes, an upcoming holiday can be related to these units, particularly if it commemorates an event in the same period you happen to be covering. Or your class may be already enthusiastic about one aspect of history in popular nonfiction or fiction. Remember Alex Haley's *Roots?* Any of these sources will provide a good framework with which to begin.

From this framework, make a list of well-known historical events during the time of your interest, unsung heroes and heroines as well as old, but curious, customs and other items of possible interest to children. Then include all of these items in mimeographed survey sheets. Or if there aren't too many items, copy this list on the board. Ask your pupils to let you know which of these items they would like to include in a class saga. To do this, have children vote with a show of hands or number items according to preference—using "1" as the first choice and "3" as the last. Which choice (item) had the most votes? Were there any other items that came close? If so, ask pupils to vote for an item they would probably enjoy working most with.

With this much done, you may now have the class work together in deciding who the characters are to be and what will happen in the saga, and allow individual children to invent their own sagas at a later time. Remind your class that these sagas are stories and should therefore have a beginning, middle and an end.

Generally, a saga tells the story of an individual, alone or as a family member, from childhood on, and his efforts to cope with a major change or problem in his life. Examples of changes may include supporting a family in hard times, building a fortune with next to nothing, or making the best of years he or she has left. The time during which these events all take place *does* matter a great deal; such as, what was the United States like about a hundred or more years ago? What kinds of conditions did people have in certain parts of the country—north, south, east or west?

Have pupils build up a saga on a small scale by imagining a particular individual or family—and combining separate stories involving just these characters. For best results, divide the class into three or four small groups to work on their character's childhood, adulthood and later years. Ask children to decide where their characters lived, what kinds of ambitions they had, what kinds of occupations they held, and how they got along in good times as well as bad. Instead of making up different characters each time, pupils will have an opportunity to find and use other details to make the saga more authentic.

Or children can write a short saga around a famous person, hero or heroine. They should try to imagine what this person would have done under different conditions. Children should also try to write the person's story as he or she might have told it to someone else.

EXPLORING COUNTRIES THROUGH FOLK TALES

With folk tales, you can enrich children's understanding of their own country and others as well. In nearly every folk tale, you and your class are bound to learn something about a particular culture's traditions, values, and views of itself. Such tales often include a culture's animals, heroes, flowers and foods in various themes.

For example, you may be familiar with U.S. folklore heroes such as Pecos Bill and Paul Bunyan, and animals such as the coyote and raven in stories of the American Indians. Although animals of nearly every kind are included in tales of other lands, you will find that bears and wolves are the most likely animals represented in Russian folklore. The fish is a frequent creature in English, German and Scandinavian stories. In African tales, a variety of animals are represented, such as crocodiles, lions, monkeys and tigers. However, you will come across Anansi the spider, Zomo the rabbit, and Ijapa the tortoise, most often. In addition to heroes and animals, tales about people, customs and leisure activities are likely to reflect a certain culture—and be most interesting to children. Topics like these will provide inspiration for a variety of different language and art learning experiences that can be adapted to nearly every grade level:

1. Compare one culture's explanation of how certain places, things or animals came to be with another's. Try using environment as an overall theme. In what ways are these explanations the same? In what ways are they different?

2. Make models of prominent animals mentioned in folk tales of a particular culture. Compare these animal's names in spelling. Try to find out what these names mean, if possible. Does this name suit the animal?

3. Build up a new set of adventures for better-known folk tale characters such as Tom Tit Tot (English), and substitute actual names of locations. Draw, paint or model your version of Tom Tit Tot.

4. Compare a hero or heroine from another culture to one of ours, such as Paul Bunyan or Casey Jones. In what ways are these heroes alike? How are they different?

5. Find or figure out how a popular folk tale such as *Hansel and Gretel* would be represented in another land. How would the children's native costumes look? How would the setting change? Would there be forests, or deserts?

6. Collect class folk tale favorites of a particular land representing such particular categories as humor, customs, plants, animals and the like.

7. Make a picture graph of different kinds of animals found in folk tales of three or four lands. Then collect some stories. Are these animals really found in these countries? What do their habitats look like? Which animals are "make-believe"? What do you think they look like? Compare your version with those of your classmates.

8. Learn names of things in the language of the country you are studying. How does each word compare with our own? Include these words in a dictionary you have made.

9. Make folk tale mobiles from small milk cartons. On each side of the carton, tape a picture of a character or

scene from a favorite folk tale. Attach a string to the top of these mobiles. Then hang them attractively from a hanger or larger cardboard carton, as in Figure 7-7.

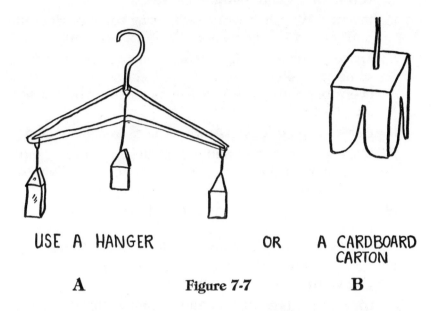

USE A HANGER   OR   A CARDBOARD CARTON

A   **Figure 7-7**   **B**

10. Make various kinds of portraits of characters from folktales, using such materials as paper bags, papier mâché, clay, crumpled newspaper, sponges, cloth or pieces of construction paper.

11. Incorporate folk tale figures and animals in such math activities as measuring (longest, shortest, thinnest, slowest, fastest), counting and problem-solving (comparing distances, etc.).

12. Put a folk tale character in a different setting or land and try to imagine the way his feelings, actions, and circumstances change. Build up another story around this character.

13. Write your own version of a tale you enjoy the most, or just change the beginning, middle or end of it and see what happens. In addition to paper and pencil, try telling your tale using dioramas, dolls, masks or shadow puppets.

14. Pretend you have a camera through which you can see

"larger than life" folk tale scenes. What would you focus your camera on? What would you see? Pretend you are making a short movie or play—what scenes do you think should follow each other?

15. Invent a folk tale of your own, using some or all of the information you know about a certain country.

16. Try to guess or think of actual names of places where some folk tales *might* have happened. Make a list of every possible place you can think of. Why did you include these places?

17. Design a set of posters for folk tales of a given land.

18. Make a collection of humorous tales found to be most popular with the class. Take a poll of the "Ten Top Funniest Tales."

19. Make up a set of extended adventures of a favorite folk tale character or person. Write these adventures for a booklet or include them in a comic-style book.

20. Play "Twenty Questions," using one or more folk tales. Use verbal hints or pantomime a scene.

21. Look at pictures of different scenes of forests, lakes, mountains, or desert of a country and try to imagine a character from any folk tale in it.

22. Mixing up various descriptions of land, animals, food, etc. in stories of other lands, try to identify the culture being referred to.

23. Tell the same tale from the main character's viewpoint. You may also wish to decide whether this character is telling the story to children, his friends, or trying to convince strangers that what he's heard is true. Suppose one of these people challenged him by asking him for proof. Think of some way to prove different things. What would happen if this proof, as such, was unacceptable? Write a new story telling about it!

8

EXPLORING THE PRESENT
SCENE AND TOMORROW

By providing a different perspective to children's experiences
and environments, you can encourage pupils to think—and have
more opportunities to use important reading and math skills.

Take the circus as a topic, for example. Certainly, it offers a
wealth of learning experiences for young children. But it has
much to offer older children as well, especially if it is seen from an
artist's viewpoint—or even as a career!

In this chapter, you will also find ways in which other old
and new topics can be adapted for classroom use. You may be
interested in a different approach to environment and ecology.
Then, perhaps, a present or future "Earth Day" is in order. Or
how about trying to imagine the future and changes that may
affect lifestyles in a big way? While the future *is* hard to predict,
children will still need to consider various alternatives—and
choose among them.

You will find many ideas in this chapter, and even think of
more as you and your class are hard at work.

MAKING THE CIRCUS THEME
WORK WITH OLDER CHILDREN

What child can resist the circus and its excitement? Visiting
the circus and seeing the clowns, acrobats, acts and animals is
always fun. So is learning about the circus in kindergarten and
primary grades—as well as upper grades! On one hand, you can
build interesting units with one or two aspects of the circus, such
as what clowns do as helpers and careers of clowns. Or you may

choose to include the whole circus in a single unit—or any combination of the following ways.

Building Around a Circus Topic

Circus careers. Find descriptions of different types of workers and the jobs they do; then use this information in activities suggested in Chapter 6. Try focusing on a few related areas of various careers, such as finding out what is learned in clown school.

Circus math. Use a circus background for math problems. In addition to simple computations and counting, experiment with imaginary proportions as well. For example, how much taller would the tall man in the circus sideshow be in a miniature circus? In a giant circus? Check these proportions out by making a large cardboard cutout of a tall man and measuring his size. (After cutting the tall man out, tape him to a handy board or wall. Use rulers, yardsticks, measuring tape, fingers, or attach paper clips to measure him. How many clips did you use? Did you use more small clips than large clips to match his height?)

As another example, try changing the sizes and shapes of tickets that are not too small (and easily lost) and not too large. Compare today's admission price with that of ten years ago. With that amount of money saved, what else could you have bought?

When the clown tries to sweep away the spotlight, it gets progressively smaller. Beginning with a drawing of a circle, figure out how to make it proportionally smaller, using a compass.

If you were responsible for buying a month's supply of food for the animals, how much would you need? How much would you probably spend?

Suppose these animals were much smaller, as in a miniature circus. Or large as giants. How much food would they need then?

Circus legends, superstitions, and stories provide insights of circus life that can be appreciated by older children. Make a list of words that describe circus life and what they mean. Use this information to compare them with some of today's descriptions. Besides dramatizing various scenes and stories, pupils can create imaginary "exposes" involving a circus happening, hero or heroine, as well as other stories and poems.

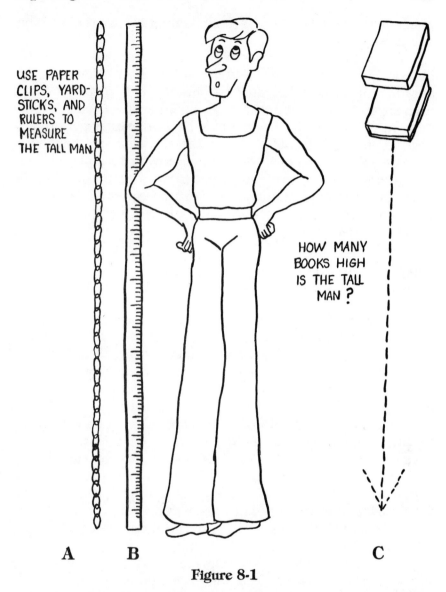

USE PAPER
CLIPS, YARD-
STICKS, AND
RULERS TO
MEASURE
THE TALL MAN.

HOW MANY
BOOKS HIGH
IS THE TALL
MAN ?

A   B   C

Figure 8-1

Circuses in history or in the future can often be included in social studies units. You might have your pupils discover what ancient Roman circuses were like or learn how Barnum and Bailey began their circus. Taking today's trends, such as rising prices, into consideration, try to imagine the circus of the future—how much money will it cost to see it or buy food and souvenirs? What will these things look like?

First find similar pictures in magazines or draw such items as balloons, banners, popcorn and hotdogs yourself. Now exaggerate their sizes and what they are meant for. Perhaps food will even shrink in size, but only a small amount will fill you up. What other means of transportation would be used to carry performers, animals and equipment? How will the animals have changed in appearance and appetites? Will the high wire be replaced? Will the clowns use different equipment to do their tricks? Will the circus be performed in outer space or underground? Divide the class into several smaller groups and assign each of these areas as topics, one per group.

Imaginary Biographies of Circus Stars, Clowns or Famous Animals

Make up a story about a circus worker of your choice—give him or her a name, his or her reasons for joining the circus and have him or her describe a few incidents that still are remembered, such as the day of the big flood or fire, the lion's escape, a clown's funny trick that turned out not to be so funny (the day the audience didn't laugh) or a humorous incident.

Travels in the circus. Trace as many possible routes for a circus to take, using a local or nationwide map. Give reasons why a circus might take such a route, along with possible advantages and disadvantages. Use the information you learned about the circus to write a saga or other long story. Include a few general descriptions of towns visited by the circus.

Come to the aid of the circus. Pretend that business has been dropping off because of inflation, unusually bad weather, and so on. You are interested in making the circus as attractive to as many people as possible, and still have a profit in the end.

Try designing a variety of promotional material before your circus reaches the next town and while it is still in town. Perhaps you can recycle some materials that would otherwise be discarded, such as previous posters, empty soda cans, burned-out light bulbs, a worn broom, and so on. Remember, too, that programs bought by the audience are advertisement for the circus. One way of making different programs is by folding a large piece of paper in half and pasting pictures cut from magazines on the borders. In the middle, write the name of your circus, its scheduled dates in your town, and a list of performances on the inside cover. An example is in Figure 8-2.

A   **Figure 8-2**   **B**

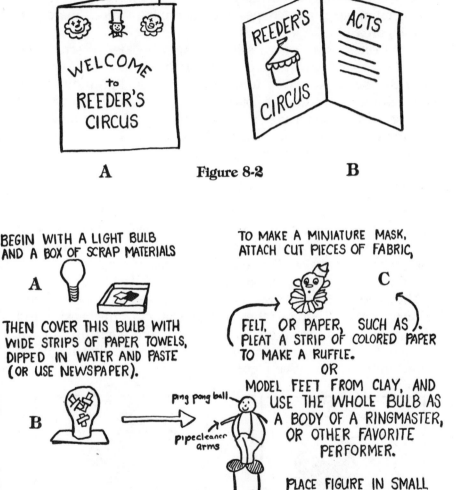

BEGIN WITH A LIGHT BULB
AND A BOX OF SCRAP MATERIALS

A

THEN COVER THIS BULB WITH
WIDE STRIPS OF PAPER TOWELS,
DIPPED IN WATER AND PASTE
(OR USE NEWSPAPER).

B

TO MAKE A MINIATURE MASK,
ATTACH CUT PIECES OF FABRIC,

C

FELT, OR PAPER, SUCH AS).
PLEAT A STRIP OF COLORED PAPER
TO MAKE A RUFFLE.
OR

MODEL FEET FROM CLAY, AND
USE THE WHOLE BULB AS
A BODY OF A RINGMASTER,
OR OTHER FAVORITE
PERFORMER.

Ping pong ball

pipecleaner arms

PLACE FIGURE IN SMALL
JUICE CAN.

Figure 8-3   **D**

Circus melodies. If possible, listen to Saint-Saens's piece, "*Carnival of Animals.*" Using the same idea, make up an original music or sound theme that might be used to let people know that the circus is coming to or leaving town. You can use a popular tune or a song you learned as background music. You can even or make up a new song dealing with the whole circus or some aspect of it.

Souvenirs. Using a single object, such as a burned-out bulb, make a circus mask, or add clay feet to make a novelty figure. Try exaggerating sizes and shapes and combining various materials. (See Figure 8-3.)

The circus as an energy saver. Make a booklet or scrapbook describing as many ways as possible for the circus to save energy. Consider such places as tents and wagons, lighting, use of supplies and water, and use of colors for better effects. How could the circus make better use of the sun and wind? What may each performer do to save energy, particularly in his or her use of circus vehicles and electrical appliances.

Making a Different Kind of Circus

Circuses in other lands. Learn about circuses in foreign countries, especially any different acts they may include. Make a list of foreign words that describe workers, animals and equipment. Then take a survey of other types of animal acts used.

Circus as seen through an artist's eyes. Splash two or three bright colors such as yellow, red and blue on a piece of cardboard or heavy paper. Then use these colors' shapes as the background of a picture of a circus scene. Draw or paint a picture, or cut pictures from magazines, of animals and people that might be found in the circus. (See Figure 8-4.)

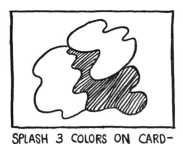

SPLASH 3 COLORS ON CARD-
BOARD.

NOW DRAW, OR CUT, PICTURES
OF ANIMALS OR PEOPLE FOUND
IN THE CIRCUS.

A   Figure 8-4   B

Experiment with cardboard, construction paper or colored cellophane shapes that represent various aspects of circus life. Or experiment with animation using film or a large disc of paper, such as shown in Figure 8-5. Draw an outline of a moving figure, such as a walking elephant. For example, on one picture, place one of the elephant's front legs ahead of the other. In succeeding pictures, change the positions of the elephant's legs so that he appears to be walking (Figure 8-5B).

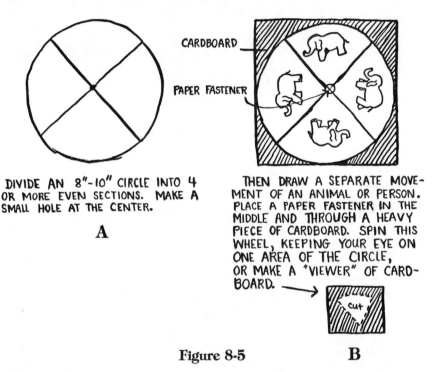

DIVIDE AN 8"-10" CIRCLE INTO 4 OR MORE EVEN SECTIONS. MAKE A SMALL HOLE AT THE CENTER.

A

THEN DRAW A SEPARATE MOVE-MENT OF AN ANIMAL OR PERSON. PLACE A PAPER FASTENER IN THE MIDDLE AND THROUGH A HEAVY PIECE OF CARDBOARD. SPIN THIS WHEEL, KEEPING YOUR EYE ON ONE AREA OF THE CIRCLE, OR MAKE A "VIEWER" OF CARD-BOARD. →

Figure 8-5 **B**

Or explore animation by drawing each movement on one sheet of paper, using about seven or more sheets of paper altogether. To make your figure "move," pretend you are looking at a booklet and flip the pages rapidly (Figure 8-6).

Circus on another planet. While circuses on earth are different in some ways and similar in others, a circus playing on another planet would be far more different than could ever be imagined. For one thing, that planet's atmosphere (if any), distance from the sun (ours or its own), and type of life can be quite unusual.

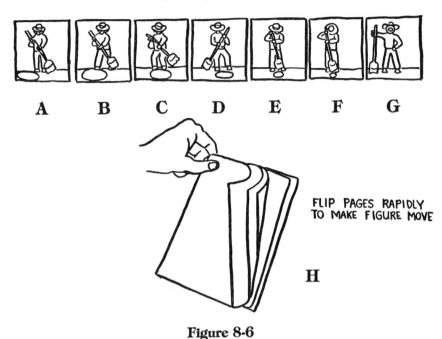

A   B   C   D   E   F   G

FLIP PAGES RAPIDLY
TO MAKE FIGURE MOVE

H

Figure 8-6

Have pupils, as a class or in small groups, choose a familiar planet or make up one. If they decide to use a real planet, pupils should first try to learn what is generally known about it. They would then have to create its physical features. For an imaginary planet, a different set of features must be invented; inhabitants and what they look like, what they do and eat, and their surroundings. The more detailed this planet is made, the more authentic children's imaginary circus will seem.

Using these facts as a general guide, children should consider the following aspects of a circus, as well as what may *not* be found in a strange setting:

- music, art
  posters
  types of tickets
- tents (if any)
- sideshow
- kinds of animals (These animals should have names and unusual shapes, colors and other characteristics. To get different names, try combining the names of two earth

animals, such as alligator and dog. One result might be "alligog.")

- performers (First decide what types of acts these creatures will do. For less confusion, name them first and provide them with specific characteristics. The more details, the more authentic these performers will seem. For example, suppose all of your performers' "legs" and "arms" are made of rubber bands? (See Figure 8-7.) Or suppose their "legs" have small magnets attached to rubber bands? Will the object of most of their tricks consist of not bending a pipe cleaner pole too far down? Because if it is, the performer will fall in a pit and keep sinking inside.)

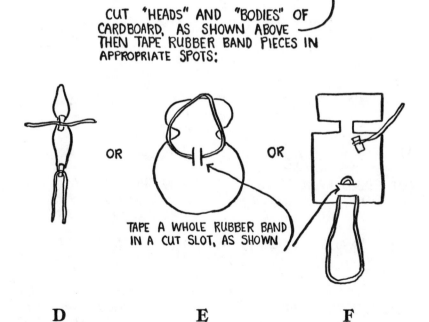

A   **B**   **C**

or   or

CUT "HEADS" AND "BODIES" OF CARDBOARD, AS SHOWN ABOVE THEN TAPE RUBBER BAND PIECES IN APPROPRIATE SPOTS:

OR   OR

TAPE A WHOLE RUBBER BAND IN A CUT SLOT, AS SHOWN

D   **E**   **F**

Figure 8-7

- kinds of circus acts (What kinds of equipment will be used by the performing creatures? What will it look like? Experiment by cutting up such items as old sponges, styrofoam and colored cellophane that may or may not resemble some of the equipment used in a circus on earth. For example, cut some of this material to look like hoops, flying trapezes, cages, stools, and so on. The shape you cut need not look like these items to the last detail—perhaps the chair has no legs, but merely crumbles away each time someone sits on it. And what if the hoop has a very wide rim and a tiny circle inside for some long, string-like animal to pass through?)

EXAMPLES OF EQUIPMENT

STYROFOAM STOOL

TURN STYROFOAM
CUP UPSIDE DOWN.

A

CUT EDGES AS
SHOWN.

B

PAINT THE
STOOL.

C

D

CUT EDGES FROM SIDES
OF AN OLD PIECE OF SPONGE.

E

USING THE POINTS OF A PAIR
OF DULL SCISSORS, PUNCH A
SMALL HOLE AT THE CENTER.

EXAMPLE OF A STRING ANIMAL

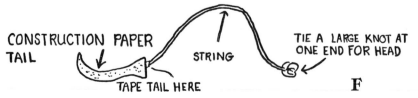

CONSTRUCTION PAPER
TAIL

STRING

TIE A LARGE KNOT AT
ONE END FOR HEAD

TAPE TAIL HERE

F

Figure 8-8

- types of measurements and currency used, if any. For example, is Base 4 or 5 used instead of Base 10? And is the length of a particular rubbery leg the basis of measuring lengths and widths? Let the children decide!
- kinds of foods these inhabitants can buy to eat as they watch the show. Or does such a custom exist on your imaginary planet?
- how animals are cared for (Again, much depends on what their bodies are made of. For example, string animals must be especially wary of sharp instruments. And animals whose bodies are cut from tracing paper also need certain kinds of care. Are these animals cared for each day, each week, or each month, or are they discarded after each performance?
- what types of energy are used, or do these inhabitants supply their own?
- experiment with colors, motion, etc. For example, by shining a flashlight on one of these strange shapes, can you get a more unusual kind of shadow? Does it seem to move? Perhaps this can be one of the "acts."

During this time, your class is likely to think of other details and put certain language and math skills to work. In addition to expressing their ideas orally and on paper, pupils will find the problem of creating new names, descriptions and other terms challenging. In math, children can test their ingenuity and skills by finding other ways to count, measure and weigh. Also, any number of art projects is possible.

Experiments should be tried with different materials for desired effects in color, shape, size and form. There are also design problems to motivate most of the children. For example, how do extraterrestrials travel from one place to another? Do they seem to shrink to the size of an atom and travel faster than the speed of light? Do they use other kinds of transportation? Do they make any use of supercomputers, or have they gone beyond that stage?

Whenever possible, try encouraging pupils to recycle such materials as scrap paper, parts of old books, magazines, string, gum wrappers, yarn, paper clips, old buttons, cardboard boxes, aluminum foil, discarded ballpoint pens, costume jewelry and candy wrappers! Other useful materials include pipe cleaners, old photographs, empty cereal boxes, plastic straws, adhesive tape, sponges, finger paint, clean milk containers, bottle caps, broken toys and alarm clocks.

As more and more projects are completed, you should consider using some type of circus atmosphere, providing still further learning opportunities, color and attractiveness. Items you might display are murals, pictures, mobiles, booklets and other things pertaining to circus life, such as models.

With these things, you may like to form various information centers about your circus. Descriptions of words invented by children, codes, math terms, games and descriptions of acts may

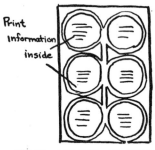

PLACE THESE PLASTIC RINGS FROM SODA CANS AGAINST A CONTRASTING PIECE OF CONSTRUCTION PAPER.

A

TAPE PLASTIC OR CARDBOARD TRAYS TOGETHER FOR A DIFFERENT BACKGROUND EFFECT.

B

ROLLED-UP CORRUGATED BOARD AROUND A WASTE BASKET IS ANOTHER GOOD FOUNDATION.

C

ARRANGE CARDBOARD CARTONS ON THE FLOOR FOR A 3-D DISPLAY. THEN TACK OR TAPE CHILDREN'S WORK ALL AROUND.

D

Figure 8-9

all be included. Such centers can be made of a piece of construction paper containing printed information, or have more elaborate foundations. Pieces of styrofoam, varying sizes of cardboard cartons, plastic rings from soda cans and bottles and rolled-up corrugated board all make good foundations of centers. Some of these foundations are shown in Figure 8-9.

COMMEMORATING EARTH DAY

In 1970, a small group of college students organized Earth Day in an effort to direct attention to pollution's effects on our environment. As a result, Earth Day was observed with a variety of activities and events across the nation—parades, speakers and seminars, teach-ins and trash-ins. Fighting pollution became an important issue of those times. And recently, pollution and conservation of natural resources are receiving more attention than ever through the media and other sources.

Certainly, most of your students may have heard of and become familiar with media messages urging them to conserve energy and fight pollution, or have learned something about these topics in previous grades.

To provide your class with another way of viewing these issues, try having pupils participate in an Earth Day commemoration of their own. Of course, this project will be on a much smaller scale and will be a more updated version of the original Earth Day. However, it will stimulate your pupils' interest and thought in the environment, and possibly motivate children to explore such related areas as energy, wildlife and weather. This project will also involve curriculum activities in science, social studies, language arts, math and art. While nearly any aspect of environment may be used as a theme in an updated version of Earth Day, the area of pollution is perhaps the most familiar to children—and the most relevant.

To give your pupils an overall perspective of pollution and our spaceship earth, try the following suggestions:

1. Collect and examine pictures of the earth as it looks in outer space. A possible source may be satellite photographs.

Using this information, make a mosaic or collage of your version of earth as a spaceship. Include pieces of aluminum foil as well as bits of dark blue, light blue, and yellow construction paper in a 5- to 6-inch circle on a lightly colored piece of heavy paper. (Use a compass to draw this circle.) Or make up poems and short written "portraits" to accompany each picture, mosaic or collage.

2. Make large charts of the different layers of the earth's atmosphere, showing where most pollution seems to be. Use diagrams found in children's books about ecology or astronomy. Have pupils find out about the "greenhouse effect" and why it is often used to describe the ultimate result of pollution. Pupils might also find comparisons of pictures of atmospheres and surfaces of Venus and Jupiter worthwhile. According to Carl Sagan, the well-known astronomer, these are extreme examples of what *may* happen to our earth if the ozone layer is destroyed.

   Have children try to imagine how this information on the greenhouse effect on the earth would be shown in an editorial carton of a newspaper or magazine. (Collect and look at a few examples of editorial cartoons first.) Then have pupils try writing an imaginary editorial column about it, calling public attention to possible dangers and urging greater awareness of and action on this situation. Run off one or two outstanding editorials and ask pupils to respond as readers to their classmates' remarks. Children may pretend to be politicians, scientists, educators, lawyers, clergy members and laypersons.

   At this point, you should encourage pupils to take a "pro" or "con" position, agreeing or disagreeing with the editor's remarks.

3. Find and try experiments about air and water pollution in children's science books.

4. Take a survey of pupils' ideas of what they think pollution means. For example, complete the following sentence: POLLUTION is _____.

5. Invent a symbol or mascot, along with a suitable slogan or warning against water, air or noise pollution.

6. "What Happens When You Pollute"—Cut separate flannel board houses, trees and outlines of polluting items, such as cars or burning garbage (as in Figure 8-10). First, arrange homes and trees to show some typical, clean sheet. Then place polluting items at various points to demonstrate how a nice-looking block can be transformed into an instant slum.

EXAMPLES

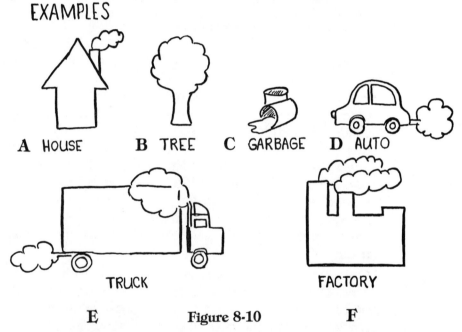

A HOUSE   B TREE   C GARBAGE   D AUTO

TRUCK   FACTORY

E   **Figure 8-10**   F

7. Make up your own version or display of a "pollution-rama" and discuss some possible improvements to clean it up. A background for a pollutionrama may be a magazine or newspaper picture of an abandoned car dump, a littered street, smokestacks emitting pollutants in the air, people blasting radios in a quiet area, or fixing cars in a residential area (complete with leaking oil, dirty rags, discarded parts on street, etc.).

8. Obtain samples of polluted water, and if possible, look at drops of this water through a microscope. Then draw

an enlarged drop of polluted water. An example is shown in Figure 8-11.

USE A SHEET OF
BLACK, BLUE, GREEN
OR BROWN CON-
STRUCTION PAPER. **A**

DRAW WHAT IS INSIDE
A DROP OF POLLUTED
WATER ON A 5"-6"
CIRCLE OF WHITE
PAPER. **B**

PASTE YOUR POLLUTED
WATER DROP ON THE
CONSTRUCTION PAPER.

C

Figure 8-11

9. Using such toys as Lincoln Logs® or other building toys, build models of devices to deal with water, air or noise pollution. Of course, these models do not have to operate, but pupils' ideas of what could be used to help clean up pollution are often ingenious. In addition to these toys, children could attach such items as paper fans or pinwheels to their structures. A written description on a small card or piece of paper should be included. It should contain the model's name, what type of pollution it takes care of, how it might operate, and what types ofp roblems it may lead to, if improperly used.

10. On a large calendar write a practical way to help your school and neighborhood remain free of trash. Picking up litter on school grounds is one possible activity. Try participating in some or all of these activities on those special days, or get someone to help you. Keep a record in pictures or writing of what you have done. Later on you may wish to include these items in a display entitled, "Every Day Is Earth Day."

11. Use the new Earth Day symbols that you have invented as button ornaments. Your button may be a jar lid, a corrugated piece of cardboard, wood or papier mâché. Or use these symbols in a poster design.

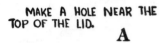

MAKE A HOLE NEAR THE TOP OF THE LID.
A

DRAW OR CUT A SUITABLE PICTURE. **B**

PASTE THIS PICTURE ON THE LID, A PIECE OF WOOD OR CARDBOARD. **C**

Figure 8-12

12. Make up a play, a short sketch, or dramatization of one aspect of your new Earth Day.

13. Find pictures and descriptions of the original Earth Day, April 22, 1970.

14. Divide the class into two groups, one group representing an industry that has been allegedly polluting the air nearby, but is the biggest source of jobs—and the other group representing concerned laypeople, environmentalists, scientists, politicians, etc. Have each group justify its stand with convincing arguments, charts or relevant magazine and newspaper pictures about pollution. Graphs might also be shown by one group for the other's benefit. Perhaps pupils will feel motivated to role-play parents, students, educators, doctors, company managers and other interested citizens. On the following day or week, ask children to change sides and argue the point from the opposite perspective.

15. Look for ways to recycle your everyday scrap materials, such as:

   • Sculpture scraps in a figure of a person or animal. Gather all discarded paper, and tie it in various forms. (See Figure 8-13.) If there is time, make these forms more permanent with papier mâché.

   • Experiment with some scrap by trying to dissolve it, or finding other ways to discard it. One way might be uncrushing all paper scraps, piling them and tying them up neatly and selling them. While you are doing that, try imagining what type of energy such scrap would make, what it would be used for and how much it would cost. Save newspaper articles that tell about attempts or pending considerations to turn trash into another source of energy.

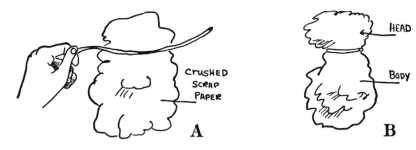

Figure 8-13

- Write about it, telling where it is commonly found, how it pollutes and what measures have been taken to clean it up. This may be a humorous description.
- Tape two or more of these items together to make a portrait of pollution, a free-form sculpture. Children are usually very clever in making such pieces.
- Use it to make a game or toy. Sometimes that stray bottle cap, string or straw can be used to replace a missing game piece, or can be part of a whole new game. Save it!

Scrap materials found in the classroom or school:

- bits of crayons, erasers, broken pencils
- scrap paper
- old workbooks, books
- cardboard trays from school lunches
- used paste and paint jars
- milk and juice containers
- boxes from school supplies, such as pencils, books, paper and learning aids
- paintbrushes
- wooden blocks, used blackboard erasers, etc.

Scrap materials usually found outside of school:

- old magazines, newspapers
- string
- bottle caps, plastic shampoo containers
- plastic straws
- broken toys
- twigs, leaves
- broken clocks
- old sponges
- old shoelaces
- discarded, clean nylon stockings
- plastic bags, cellophane
- empty match covers
- discarded wallets, purses, wristwatch bands
- junk mail, including contents of some of it, and en-velopes
- cereal box cardboard
- discarded plastic containers
- spools, odd remnants of fabric

16. *Earth Day Game.*

    How to Make:

    1. On a large piece of cardboard, say 18 × 20 inches, draw the game board as shown in Figure 8-14B. For easier use, plan to make each section-square about 1¼ inches.
    2. Print all directions. Then protect your board after painting or decorating by having it laminated, or cover it with clear, self-sticking plastic.
    3. Using a compass, draw a circle about 4 or 5 inches on a 6 × 6-inch square of cardboard. Copy letters as shown in Figure 8-14A. Then cut out this circle and make a hole at its center—large enough for a paper fastener to go through.
    4. Attach spinner to the foundation cardboard by push-ing the fastener through its center hole and the

cardboard underneath. To make this wheel spin more freely, turn it around in both directions so that the hole will be the right size. Then try using it the way a child would. Repeat this process, if necessary.

5. For markers, use buttons, bottle caps, charms or cardboard circles. You will need one for each of two players.

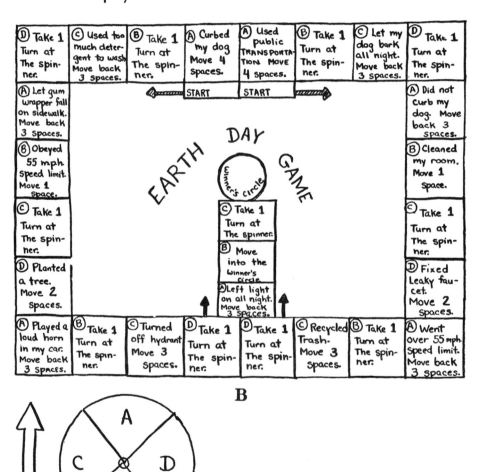

Figure 8-14

How to Play:

1. Two players at a time may use this game.
2. After choosing markers, each player places his or her marker in one of the boxes marked "Start."
3. The first player spins the spinner and places his or her marker in the first box corresponding with the letter indicated by the pointer. The second player takes a turn.
4. Each time a play is made, the immediate set of letters is always used next. However, if a player lands on a space marked "Move back 2 spaces" or something to that effect, he or she moves to the letter set immediately before the set he or she reached.
5. In playing, one player moves to the left and the other to the right, as indicated by the arrows on the game board.
6. The player reaching the winner's circle first is the winner.
7. For easier playing, you may wish to make each set of letters—A, B, C, D—a different color. That is, the set of letters following the word, "Start" may be blue, the following set, yellow, and so on. This color code will be less confusing to the players.

SEEING SOCIETIES THROUGH SCIENCE FICTION: MAKING A DIFFERENT ENVIRONMENT

According to writers like Asimov, there are different categories of science fiction. One popular category deals with space adventures, another with gadgets, and still another with alternative societies. Some children may have even seen movies featuring all kinds of stories about outer space and are quite familiar with unusual settings as well as happenings. On the other hand, few children may be aware that certain technological, social and environmental changes result in many kinds of settings. Social science fiction explores these numerous possibilities. For example, can children imagine what kind of living is possible in an ice, sand or even garbage-filled country? Or what happens to the environment when every trace of wildlife is gone? Suppose no changes happened for a long period of time?

At any rate, children will have to learn to choose wisely from various alternatives as adults—and how to cope with previous changes in the environment. Considering possible changes, or what *might* happen on our earth or other planet, is a good way to begin with science fiction as a tool. First, look through a few science fiction novels and stories written for children. Try reading one or more of them, if possible. You will certainly want to write down titles and authors of suitable books for later reference. Then borrow some of these books and display them in your classroom library. Whenever you can, try including titles that relate to your present science and social studies units.

By doing this, you will motivate your pupils to read *and think*. Be sure to allow enough time for pupils to read and even discuss various science fiction books. Vary children's science fiction reading with related activities described in this chapter. In addition to having pupils making dioramas, doing simple experiments and inventing other stories, you will find useful suggestions in previous chapters of this book. True, children will become familiar with science fiction in general. But they will also gain ideas about alternative societies as well and feel encouraged to participate in a simulation of some imaginary, but possible, environment. Pupils will be creating a setting of their own.

Once children are familiar with science fiction, they will think of different choices and possibilities with more ease. Their first experiment should be close to their own experiences, such as pretending that comfortable weather is possible all year long, or imagining how to live without certain conveniences for about fifty years or more. For now, however, pupils should try to think how this situation may change next week, next month or even next year, as well as possible advantages and disadvantages. Later on, children should extend what they already know about this situation to specific things, like the situation's effect at home, at school, on different jobs and on outdoor environments.

Then stop at this point and have interested volunteers work together in small groups. One group might develop background scenery (murals, for instance). Another group might make models of various kinds of buildings using all types of cartons, and so on. Perhaps some children can think how items like toys or transportation would look in their new environment.

Each group should make a record of their ideas, using different kinds of lists, booklets, pictures and paintings, descriptions on 3 × 5-inch cards and drawings.

During this time, you may have younger pupils work with a very simple environment. In other words, you can have children pretend that elements such as trees are permanently missing and think of what the consequences would be. With older pupils, you will enjoy extending learning experiences in language arts, social studies and science in the guidelines suggested below.

Social Studies

Write a history of your imaginary environment, describing what it was like before these changes took place, what alternatives were available, and were eventually taken, and why. You may also include the reactions of a cross section of people, like politicians, laypersons, scientists, lawyers, artists, environmentalists, technicians, salespeople, business managers, secretaries and file clerks. If these people had their way, what would they have done? Instead of writing these reactions on papers, try a fifteen-minute imaginary radio broadcast. Naturally, you should consider what type of radios will be used, or change them altogether and call them something else.

Or why not write a contemporary magazine or newspaper article describing how people in general are living with these changes and what they have already done to the environment? Make up a family or individual budget sample for your imaginary setting or describe what new jobs are available at this time. In the end, you may wish to include reports of any remaining natural resources and any new synthetic materials. Remember, also, to invent a name for your newspaper or magazine.

Science

Describe and design different forms of transportation in your new environment, inventing names for each one. As a further guide, consider looking at pictures of developments of earlier cars, trains and airplanes. Then think what could be added, subtracted or even changed. Try thinking of how the weather conditions might have changed, or still are in the process of changing. Invent a new technological item by using some of our present items. For example, how would an automatic duster work? What would it look like? How much would it cost? Draw, paint or make models of new kinds of plants and animals in your imaginary environment.

One way of doing this is by experimenting with clay forms. Remember that none of your new forms should resemble familiar trees, flowers or animals. Once you have these things, classify them according to color, weight, height, function and other physical features. Think of new ways to conserve especially useful plants and animals you have invented.

Art

Make a large mural for the classroom of one or two background scenes of your imaginary setting. Items of interest, such as pictures of buildings and their interiors, transportation, toys, inventions and smaller conveniences, may be included. What kinds of entertainment exist in your new environment? What kinds of music and dance would there be? What things would you include in your environment's imaginary museum? As a guide, consider what items you would include from the present time in such a museum. How would you describe a camera, for example, to answer a puzzled descendant's questions?

Language Arts

Look over items you have invented and make sure you have names for them. Write your own reactions to the whole scene in an essay or booklet entitled, "Letter to the Editor," or express them in the words of a song. Choose one of those new jobs you invented in your new environment. Then write a journal of your daily routine for three days or a week. Predict what changes are in store for your invented environment, using a "crystal ball" or other approach.

WHAT WILL THE FUTURE BE LIKE?

Whether you realize it or not, you probably teach about the future in many ways. Perhaps you used practical activities to help your pupils become more aware of their community *and* environment in general. Or maybe you involved children in planning upcoming trips and class plays, or even introduced your class to science fiction and such related topics as alternate societies. While all of these activities are future-oriented, they can be greatly enhanced by teaching about the future itself. True, no one can really predict the future, but every pupil can certainly try imagining several different futures. In doing so, they can learn to think about possible alternatives from which to choose.

In the beginning, try having pupils use various words and ways to describe what the word "future" means to them personally, extending these descriptions as much as possible. For example, go into specific details of the future in terms of:

- tomorrow
- next week
- next month
- next year
- 5 years from now
- 10 years from now

Some possible activities may include:

1. *Making a personal time line of one possible (personal) future.* On a long strip of paper, measure and label some or all of the periods of time mentioned above. Then write what *might* happen in each section and some of

Figure 8-15

the possible effects on society. Try dramatizing the "length" of time in each section, using Figure 8-15 as a guide.

2. *Including class definitions and descriptions of the future in a booklet.* Encourage your pupils to use magazine pictures, scrap materials and even individual words accompanied by written definitions and line drawings. Place students' work in a large loose leaf binder, label and display this book in your classroom library or creative writing center. Such a book can also serve as an idea book for stories and other artwork. For further inspiration, take a look at some of Paul Klee's drawings and paintings. What do they seem to suggest?

3. *Allow pupils to experiment in making various simple predictions.* For example, make a miniature learning or question center from a small cardboard box and include questions and examples of types of predictions that can be made. See directions in Figure 8-16. In using all of these items, pupils should be able to find out whether some of their predictions are correct or not. Examples of such items include dice, spinners, (child would predict

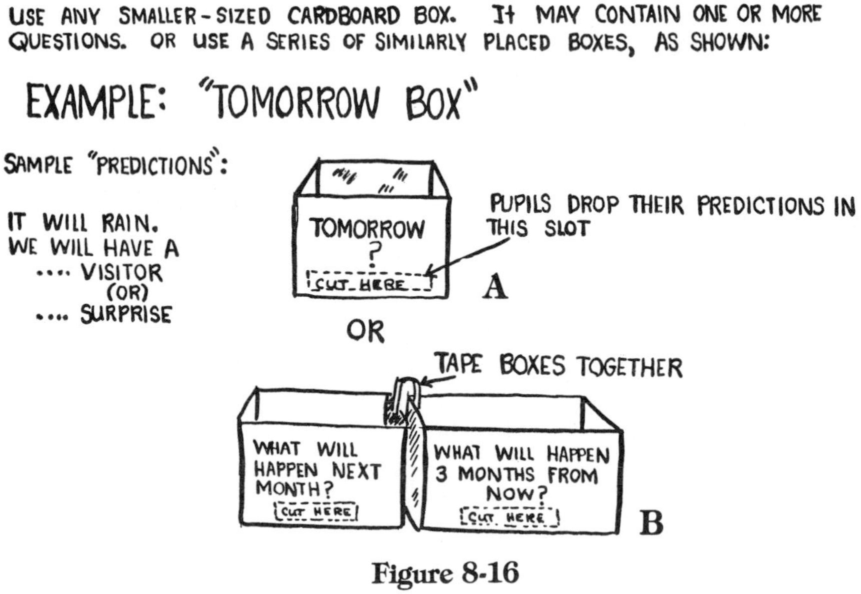

USE ANY SMALLER-SIZED CARDBOARD BOX. IT MAY CONTAIN ONE OR MORE QUESTIONS. OR USE A SERIES OF SIMILARLY PLACED BOXES, AS SHOWN:

EXAMPLE: "TOMORROW BOX"

SAMPLE "PREDICTIONS":

IT WILL RAIN.
WE WILL HAVE A
···· VISITOR
    (OR)
···· SURPRISE

TOMORROW
?
CUT HERE

PUPILS DROP THEIR PREDICTIONS IN THIS SLOT

A

OR

TAPE BOXES TOGETHER

WHAT WILL HAPPEN NEXT MONTH?
CUT HERE

WHAT WILL HAPPEN 3 MONTHS FROM NOW?
CUT HERE

B

Figure 8-16

what would appear "heads up" on the dice, or where the pointer in a spinner would show), tic-tac-toe games, and perhaps illustrations of checker or chess games in progress. Here, the child would not only have to predict what the next move would be, but would have to anticipate what move to make in return. (See Figure 8-17.)

SPINNERS:

SPONGE DICE:

A

WHITE RED
PURPLE GREEN
ORANGE YELLOW
BLUE

C

TAPE ON CUT-OUTS OF CIRCLES, TRIANGLES, ETC., ON EACH SIDE

ERASER DICE:

B

6 4 7
2 O
1 8 3

USE A COMPASS AND CARDBOARD FOR THESE

D

54
26

WRITE A NUMBER IN INK ON EACH SIDE.

Figure 8-17

In addition to these games, include line figure drawings, such as those shown in Figure 8-18, on 3 × 5-inch cards. Children would then try predicting which way their classmate would turn a card. To use, cards are placed face down. The first player would pick up the top card and, shielding it from his classmate, turn it in a certain way: left, right, up, down, etc. After he or she tells a classmate what the drawing looks like (before it was moved), the other child would indicate which way that card was turned. Then he or she would be allowed to see which way it was turned, learning at the same time whether or not he or she was correct.

POSSIBLE FIGURES

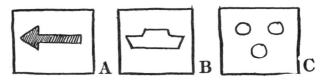

OR TRY THE FOLLOWING:

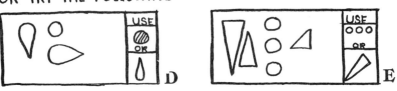

CREATE A DIFFERENT PATTERN BY TRYING TO OUTGUESS A CLASSMATE. DRAW THE FIGURE (ONE FIGURE FROM "USE" COLUMN) YOU THINK HE OR SHE CHOSE.

Figure 8-18

Or have pupils use an egg timer and try to see how many simple activities can be related to performing a few simple tasks within a certain limit, say a minute or less. When that time is up, children should discover just how much of their predictions were correct—and use this information on a graph.

Possible activities:

- writing one's name
- watering a plant
- drawing a straight line
- taking the eraser from the blackboard and placing it on one's desk

- counting up to 20 (or other given number)
- working out 3, 4, or 5 arithmetic examples on paper
- coloring a picture
- looking at, and writing, what time it is
- bouncing a ball once
- putting pencils, pens, or papers in the desk
- finding a certain given page in a given book
- writing the name of one thing that can be seen from the window
- drawing a simple design
- putting a card game back in order
- picking a scrap of paper from the floor
- writing down the name of one favorite television program, color, book, article of clothing or toy
- using toy money, making change of a dollar, quarter or fifty cents
- converting an English measurement into metrics or vice versa
- tying a shoelace
- buttoning a sweater
- rolling a sleeve up or down
- quickly naming one farm or zoo animal
- tying a bow
- touching your toes
- placing your notebook on the desk
- making a clay ball
- hanging up a picture

Or place slips of paper in a small paper bag with individual messages such as "sing," "sit down" or "stand tall." Then have pupils predict what their message will be. They should be encouraged to keep a record of correct predictions, and allowed to decide whether they wish to obey the command or not.

4. *Experimenting with predictions in typical situations.*
Have small groups of pupils participating in "thinking
ahead" games and exploring various alternatives at the
same time. Try using the following examples:

- You have planned a picnic about three weeks
from now, right down to the last detail. In what
ways will you have to change your plans and/or
activities?

- You are sure that a certain school project can be
completed by the time the weekend is over, and
think you have taken care of all the necessary details. What are some of the things that can happen
in the meantime, enabling you to finish the project ahead of time? Or what could delay this project to the very last minute? What would your
choices be in either example? You promised your
friends that you would be at the field to substitute
for the shortstop or quarterback who was unable
to play all of a sudden. Or perhaps you and your
friends agreed to meet at another friend's house
before seeing a movie. Try thinking of everything
that might happen in the meantime, as well as all
the possible choices you have in the matter.

- One of your friends, sisters or brothers has bor-
rowed one of your sweaters, books or games and
still has not returned that item. You are interested
in getting this item back in the easiest way possible, and still be on good terms with this person.
What are some of the things you can do?

- You are reading a mystery book and find a page
missing in the middle of the story. This page was
probably all you needed to solve the mystery by
yourself. At least it seemed to have contained
some important information (a friend told you
this). The library does not have another copy of
the book and your friend has since moved away.
What are some of the choices open to you? Which

one would you pick, and why? What do you think will happen after that choice is made?

- *Play the "Because" Game.* One or more players can take part, either orally or using 3 × 5-inch cards. One player begins by saying, "Because there was no other place to dump garbage, the city enlarged the present dump." The next player continues with something like the following, "Because the dump was larger, more and more garbage was thrown in it from neighboring communities." Players take turns until they exhaust possible consequences and alternatives. Players can extend this game by reading and researching the political, social, environmental and technological aspects of this situation; then playing the game once more, using the information they have gained. Instead of individual players, perhaps two opposing teams of pupils could present their own sides of such consequences. The side who presents the most sound and logical reasons is the winner.

HAVING FUN WITH PREDICTIONS

1. Make a list of things, such as hairstyles, toys, money, vehicles or sports, and try to predict how different these items will look about ten years from now. Try thinking in terms of future expenses, shapes and sizes, and if these items will be improved or allowed to disappear from use altogether.

2. Write a how-to booklet or folder for some future or present time, entitled, "How *You* Can Prevent Future Shock." (You can have pupils read excerpts from Alvin Toffler's book, *Future Shock.*)

3. Find as many new words or expressions for things and terms in use today. You may wish to include popular expressions, such as "What's happening?" and so on.

Write how your descendants might interpret these and other words or expressions. Do you think any of these terms will be unheard of years from now? What do you think their replacements will be? To understand how this works, look in history books or very old dictionaries for quaint words or terms that might have been popular a long time ago. Are any of these words still in use, or have their meanings changed? Are any of these words still the same?

4. Make up, or find examples of trends in fashions, music, art, and so on, that seemed to have been slowly accepted and finally became big hits or failures.

5. Using the suggestions included in "Making Different Environments," try predicting what will happen to such familiar settings as the bottom of the ocean, jungle, desert or mountaintop.

6. *Exaggerated Forecasts.* Have pupils pretend that the President or other high official makes one or more predictions. Given a number of situations, how would his or her forecast change by the time a week had passed? A month? A year? After imagining what such politicians had predicted, invent circumstances that would change any or all of these predictions in some way. Would that official have been better off had he or she made no prediction at all? Or having made this prediction, did this person have at least some foresight to deal with actual circumstances?

7. At the beginning of the new television season, make a prediction about one of the newest programs and compare this prediction with what eventually happens. Use what you have learned to invent as many kinds of lessons (to be learned from this story) as possible.

8. Pretend that you are writing a letter to someone in the past. In this letter, include any changes that you feel would surprise this particular person a great deal, especially if this person was a farsighted thinker. To make this activity especially interesting, pretend to be someone of a future date writing to a person living in the

present year. What are some possible changes that might have taken place?

9. Using a favorite science fiction story, write a different ending and predict what happens after all of the problems seem to be solved.

10. Predict as many different futures as you can, making each one as unusual as possible. Then extend each future by thinking of its consequences on society and the environment as a whole.

9

UNIQUE TEACHING UNITS THAT ADD SPARK TO LESSON PLANS

Many times, that so-called "old topic" can be explored from a different perspective. After providing an overall view of ancient Egypt, for example, try focusing on some aspect of the Old, Middle or New Kingdoms. Perhaps the name Tutankhamen sounds familiar to some of your pupils. If so, you will find that it is a good starting point to use in building an interesting study of ancient Egypt, and this chapter shows you how to begin. Or you may be developing a transportation unit. In this unit, you can increase pupils' interest by including trains as a separate or related topic. On the other hand, try enhancing various areas of the curriculum by relating them to such topics as magic, the mystery of Stonehenge or a "behind-the-scenes" look at television—all found in this chapter.

KING TUT LIVES AGAIN!

As you probably know, the mummy of King Tutankhamen was found intact by Howard Carter and Lord Carnovan in 1922, along with other objects of interest. While these artifacts provided some insights of what life was like during Tutankhamen's short reign, very little was discovered about the king himself. However, what is known to date about King Tutankhamen is interesting. For example, the king's name, originally spelled Tutankhaten, (in honor of the god Aten) was changed with the ruler's cult, to Tutankhamen (in honor of the god Amen). In addition to this and other meager information about the king, other areas of life in the New Kingdom are worthwhile sources of various activities, such as the following:

1. Read about some of the problems Howard Carter faced in unearthing the tomb, cleaning and sorting its many objects, preserving the condition of such objects and protecting them against theft. Pretend to be one of the helpers or close assistants of Carter's expedition. Use words or pictures to tell about the day that Tutankhamen's tomb was discovered. Or do any of the following:

   • Make up an oral or written dialogue between Carter and one of his men. Pretend that Carter has discovered that this helper is eager to tell about the tomb's contents to a close friend. Have him persuade this helper to keep the secret, explaining why secrecy is still necessary (because much more work remains to be done, etc.).

   • Make up various programs and posters that might have been displayed at the time of Carter's announcement of King Tut's tomb.

   • Pretend to be an important visitor at the tomb site. Describe who you are, any maps or invitations (even government orders) you may have received to inspect the tomb, and items you have seen that impress you the most. Or imagine that you are a curator from an important foreign or American museum and are trying to picture how some of the objects could enhance your museum's Egyptian room. To do this, first learn what a museum curator does. Then pretend you are looking at each object in turn through a viewer. What kinds of objects would you include in your museum's collection if you were given the authority to make a choice—and were able to negotiate with the Egyptian government?

   • Make up a story about the discovery of the tomb site, perhaps involving a rival expedition or strange happenings.

    • Learn what modern archaeologists do, and the training needed for such work.

2. Pretend to be a news reporter who is covering the discovery of Tutankhamen's tomb. Or be a modern-day TV newsperson covering an up-to-date report of a new discovery in the vicinity of the tomb site. Invent a possible discovery and tell about it.

3. As an archaeologist or helper on Carter's expedition, write about the sensations you may have felt upon entering the tomb for the very first time. Include your own impressions of the idea of breathing dust that is about 3,000 years old, along with different smells, noises, whispers and such discomforts as the heat and swarming insects—in a letter to a friend or someone in your family.

4. On sheets of wrapping paper or separate sheets of paper bags taped together, draw stick figures in pictures of hunting and fishing episodes that officials during Tutankhamen's reign might have enjoyed and participated in (Figure 9-1).

Figure 9-1

5. As intruders plundered a tomb, they sometimes defaced its walls and corridors with graffiti. What would they have written, for example, after an unsuccessful attempt to reach Tutankhamen's inner tomb, had there been sufficient time? Do you think archaeologists would find this graffiti helpful, or at least, interesting? What do you think future archaeologists would make of our present-day graffiti? What kind of impression would these people have of this western civilization?

6. Write separate statements, both true and false, about some aspect of ancient Egyptian life during the reign of

the New Kingdom on separate slips of paper. Place all of these slips in a paper bag or box lid. Each player draws a slip from this bag without peeking. If that player answers a statement by correctly identifying it as true or false, that player receives one point. Subtract a point for each incorrect answer.

7. Design different kinds of postcards showing one or more scenes of ancient Egypt during Tutankhamen's times, objects from his tomb or interesting places of modern-day Egypt. Pupils should try researching some of this material in books about Egypt, obtaining folders from the Egyptian Tourist Office in New York, or writing to a pen pal organization to obtain the name of an Egyptian pen pal.

ACTIVITIES FOR ANCIENT EGYPT

1. Keep a record of all stereotypes of ancient Egypt you have heard, read about and seen. Do this by keeping lists, saving cartoons and pictures, or drawing various pictures by yourself. Include a category for each list, such as "Clothing," "Mummies," "Homes," and so on. For example, commoners' "kilts" were worn differently around the waist. Some of these kilt-like garments may have been merely wrapped around the waist and tied in front, while others may have included a pleat here or there. To learn more, try visiting a museum and looking at models and pictures of ancient Egyptian dress.

2. Try finding pictures of stamp seals used in the XVIII Dynasty in texts and look at the ways in which animals such as cats, ducks and hedgehogs were represented. Look for pictures of representations of hippos, frogs and fish. Using potato halves, Play Doh, pieces of clay or corks, design other kinds of seals (using animals) that Egyptians might have used. (See Figures 9-2 and 9-3.) Make a catalog of various seals you have invented and include what they can be used on and by whom. Give your reader new insights by writing related stories and myths about your imaginary seals.

SEALS

POTATOES:

A CUT POTATOES IN HALF.

B OUTLINE THE SHAPE OF AN ANIMAL ON ONE OF THESE HALVES. REMEMBER TO KEEP IT SIMPLE.

C USING THE DULL EDGE OF A KNIFE OR SCISSORS, GENTLY SCRAPE AWAY THE BACKGROUND BEHIND THE FIGURE UNTIL THE FIGURE SEEMS TO STAND OUT.

MODEL PLAY DOH OR USE CORKS IN THE WAY SHOWN ABOVE.

Figure 9-2

USE PRINTING INK OR DYE.   PRESS FIGURE GENTLY IN IT, AND STAMP YOUR DESIGN ON PAPER, CLOTH, OR CARDBOARD.

A   **B** IT MAY ALSO BE HELPFUL TO EXAGGERATE PARTS OF ANIMAL'S BODY TO GET A BETTER DESIGN.

Figure 9-3

3. Find pictures of ancient Egyptian boats and, using these pictures as guides, make models of such forms of transportation. One simple, effective way to make an Egyptian river boat consists of rolling eight separate 4 × 10-inch sheets of newspaper in separate rolls. Place these rolls side by side and bind their ends by weaving strong cord around them. Finally, bind the middle part of the boat in the same way, and you will have a rough approximation of an ancient Egyptian river boat. Add figures made of clay for a more "life-like" effect. Figure 9-4 shows you how to make the river boat.

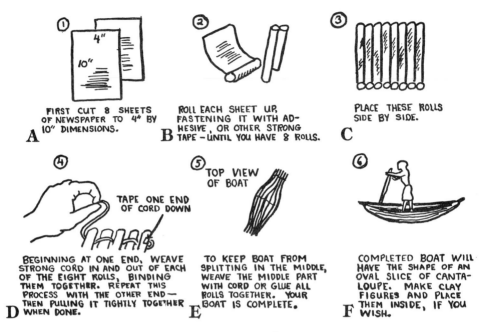

① FIRST CUT 8 SHEETS
OF NEWSPAPER TO 4" BY
10" DIMENSIONS.
A

② ROLL EACH SHEET UP,
FASTENING IT WITH AD-
HESIVE, OR OTHER STRONG
B TAPE - UNTIL YOU HAVE 8 ROLLS.

③ PLACE THESE ROLLS
SIDE BY SIDE.
C

④ TAPE ONE END
OF CORD DOWN
BEGINNING AT ONE END, WEAVE
STRONG CORD IN AND OUT OF EACH
OF THE EIGHT ROLLS, BINDING
THEM TOGETHER. REPEAT THIS
PROCESS WITH THE OTHER END —
THEN PULLING IT TIGHTLY TOGETHER
D WHEN DONE.

⑤ TOP VIEW
OF BOAT
TO KEEP BOAT FROM
SPLITTING IN THE MIDDLE,
WEAVE THE MIDDLE PART
WITH CORD OR GLUE ALL
ROLLS TOGETHER. YOUR
E BOAT IS COMPLETE.

⑥ COMPLETED BOAT WILL
HAVE THE SHAPE OF AN
OVAL SLICE OF CANTA-
LOUPE. MAKE CLAY
FIGURES AND PLACE
THEM INSIDE, IF YOU
F WISH.

Figure 9-4

4. Look at a map of ancient Egypt, preferably one that includes cities which existed during the reign of Tutankhamen, or the times of the New Kingdom. As you probably know, most Egyptian travel within the country was limited, even for native Egyptians! Allowing for this, draw another map that includes some possible imaginary road routes for visitors, tradesmen and government officials. For example, what would be the shortest route for a tradesman to follow between two cities; a large city and some imaginary town?

5. Take the part of a rich landowner, a government official or commoner and figure out what items you could use in bartering for some desired item. Use role-playing to bargain orally with another classmate assuming the same, higher or lower rank.

6. Play a simple version of an ancient Egyptian board game. First copy the version in Figure 9-5 on a large piece of cardboard, about the size of a pizza carton.

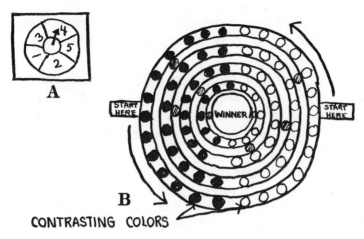

CONTRASTING COLORS

Figure 9-5

To Make:

For drawing even-sized circles, you will find that a compass works best. However, you can try experimenting with jar lids, plates and lids of various sizes. Be sure to include each detail, as shown. As you color this game board, use contrasting colors for opposite sides. Such colors will look especially effective on a neutral background, say beige, gray, or a pale shade of green, blue or pink.

You will also need two different kinds of markers, one for each of two players. Buttons, bottle caps, cardboard circles, charms, corks and egg carton cups (cut to size) all make good markers. Use dice or make a spinner (as shown) for players to use.

To Play:

Each player places his marker in spaces with the words, "Start Here," and uses the spinner or dice to find out how many spaces to advance his marker. The second player follows the same procedure. Then play is continued until one of the players reaches the "winner's circle" at the center of the board. Players may move to the next inner circle on this board when their markers are closest to the large shaded circles shown

on the board. (They can move in as they are counting—
they do not have to land on the "adjoining" space by
exact count.)

Another classroom version of this game involves
practicing reading or math skills. In order to move
ahead in this game, a player must be able to read a
certain word or give the correct answer to a math problem.

Of course, the ancient Egyptians left no written instructions on how to play a game of this type. We can
only guess. But it is fun to imagine how such game
might have been played, and that is why a version of it
is included here.

7. Have pupils make models of elephants, dogs, mice,
   camels, cows and cats, while varying the shapes of
   these animals for interesting effects. You may find that
   asking children to find many different pictures of these
   animals *before* modeling them is a good idea. In addition to clay, pupils may cut out cardboard animals with
   movable parts. That is, drawing the body of an animal
   separately from such parts as heads and legs. The animal would be assembled with paper fasteners.

8. A favorite Egyptian pet, the cat, was often depicted in
   various paintings and sculptures as well as the goddess
   Bastet. After looking at pictures of *Bastet*, make up a
   myth about cats that an adult might have told to a child
   in ancient Egyptian times.

9. Use beads to form floral designs. To make beads, roll
   4-inch long strips (¼-inch wide) of wet newspaper
   dipped in paste around short pieces of wire, bobby pins
   or straightened paper clips, as shown in Figures 9-6A
   and 9-6B. Make about 25-30 beads. After allowing them
   to dry, paint them and arrange them in a floral pattern
   by threading them on string or thin wire, and bending
   each strand into a design. (See Figure 9-6C.)

10. For role-playing and perhaps a class play about ancient
    Egypt, you may find that a helmet that may have been
    worn by Tutankhamen will be useful. Make a simple

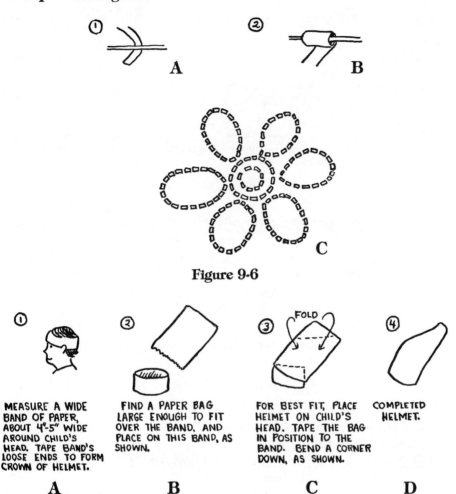

Figure 9-6

① MEASURE A WIDE BAND OF PAPER, ABOUT 4"-5" WIDE AROUND CHILD'S HEAD. TAPE BAND'S LOOSE ENDS TO FORM CROWN OF HELMET.

② FIND A PAPER BAG LARGE ENOUGH TO FIT OVER THE BAND, AND PLACE ON THIS BAND, AS SHOWN.

③ FOR BEST FIT, PLACE HELMET ON CHILD'S HEAD. TAPE THE BAG IN POSITION TO THE BAND. BEND A CORNER DOWN, AS SHOWN.

④ COMPLETED HELMET.

A   B   C   D

Figure 9-7

version of such a helmet by following the directions in Figure 9-7.

11. To really appreciate hieroglyphics as a form of writing art, have children make up a character using pen and ink, poster paint or pencil and paper. An example is shown in Figure 9-8. Then use this or another character as a design motif in jewelry, bookcovers, bookmarks or key chains. This is one way to introduce pupils to simple aspects of calligraphy. At another time, look at examples of how the alphabet can be written: long, graceful letters; short, "heavy" letters, etc.

HORUS, OR HIS LIKENESS, IS OFTEN USED IN
HIEROGLYPHICS.

Figure 9-8

12. Investigate the type of math computations performed
by ancient Egyptians and teach simpler ones to children. There is an excellent description of Egyptian math
in Barbara Mertz's book, *Red Land, Black Land* (Dodd,
Mead, & Co., New York, 1978). You might consult this
fine book for a more detailed description of other aspects of ancient Egyptian life. In addition, try the following children's books for further information and ideas:

Children's Books

Boase, Wendy, *Ancient Egypt,* Gloucester Press, New York, 1978.

Leacroft, Helen and Richard, *The Buildings of Ancient Egypt,* William
Scott, New York, 1963.

Miller, Shane and Ochsenschlager, Edward, *Life Long Ago: The Egyptians,* Coward, McCann, New York, 1963.

Perl, Lila, *Egypt: Rebirth on the Nile,* William Morrow & Co., New York,
1977.

Pine, Tillie, and Levine, Joseph, *The Egyptians Knew,* McGraw-Hill,
New York, 1964.

Books for Teachers

Hoving, Thomas, *Tutankhamun: The Untold Story,* Simon and Schus-
ter, New York, 1978.

Johnson, Paul, *The Civilization of Ancient Egypt,* Atheneum, New York,
1978.

Ruffle, John, *The Egyptians,* Phaedon Press, Oxford, England, 1977.

13. Make different kinds of masks of Tutankhamen and other famous ancient Egyptians with various materials. First find pictures of Egyptian masks. Then model your own version of Tutankhamen's and others with clay on cardboard—for strictly ornamental purposes, or as a foundation for papier mâché. Other mask possibilities include paper bags (draw and color a face on bag), pie plates, sections of cardboard cartons and crushed aluminum foil placed over poster board outlines. See directions in Figure 9-9 for pie plates and cardboard cartons.

PIE PLATES:

TURN A PIE PLATE UPSIDE DOWN.

DRAW A CIRCLE ON A PIECE OF HEAVY PAPER OR CONSTRUCTION PAPER AND CUT IT OUT. (MAKE THIS CIRCLE THE SAME SIZE AS THAT ON THE PAPER PLATE.

AFTER DRAWING ON FEATURES, GLUE OR TAPE MASK TO CIRCLE ON THE PIE PLATE. MAKE TWO SMALL HOLES ON EITHER SIDE OF THE PLATE. THREAD A PIECE OF STRING THROUGH. YOUR MASK IS COMPLETE.

A **B** **C**

CARDBOARD BOXES:

ARRANGE SMALL BOXES OF VARIOUS SIZES FOR PROMINENT FEATURES OF THIS GIANT MASK. TAPE THEM TO-GETHER WITH ADHESIVE TAPE.

PLACE ALUMINUM FOIL OR WRAPPING PAPER OVER THESE BOXES, MOLDING IN FEATURES AS YOU WORK.

CUT FEATURES, SUCH AS EYES AND HEADDRESS FROM CONSTRUCTION PAPER. GLUE OR TAPE THESE FEATURES ON MASK. PLACE YOUR MASK IN A LARGER BOX LID AND USE IT IN A TABLE DISPLAY.

D **E** **F**

Figure 9-9

MAGIC AND WITCHCRAFT

Magic is very old. Certainly, it was an important part of many ancient cultures, all the way down to more recent times, from medicine men to modern magicians. In one way or another, these magicians had to put on a convincing performance to show that a spell, cure, or even a trick "worked." Sometimes, very little magic, if any, was used. For example, today's magicians rely more on sleight-of-hand tricks than actual magic in entertaining audiences.

But magic as such can go beyond images of these and other kinds of magicians for it involves the whole world of fantasy, or make-believe in stories, daydreams and poems. *Alice in Wonderland, Snow White, The Sorcerer's Apprentice* and Tolkien's *Hobbit* are a few examples of this kind of fantasy. In children's imaginations, anything and everything is possible—water that changes to ice, ink that disappears and flashing lightning all seem to appear "by magic." While magic can be quite appealing to children, you may find that it has much to offer, particularly in the language arts.

EXPLORING THE WORLD OF MAKE-BELIEVE

In addition to using any or all of the following "what-ifs" in creative writing, poems and dramatizations, try relating them to math concepts (lengths, widths, counting, fractions and other measurements), crafts (puppets, models of figures, etc.) and science (such as research on what makes airplanes fly, what the moon's surface really looks like and simple physics experiments). Children's books are especially good sources to check first, if only for their clear explanations and helpful diagrams.

- if animals could talk
- if you could be invisible whenever you wished
- if fairies were real
- if your every wish came true
- if you could keep a top or pinwheel spinning forever
- if your room cleaned itself
- if raindrops could turn to real pennies
- if your nose grew long like Pinocchio's each time you said something that wasn't true
- if you could fly on a magic carpet
- if money appeared in your wallet each time you spent some change

- if everything you wanted was free
- if summer (or any other favorite season) never ended
- if you were able to live on the moon
- if trees and flowers grew up instantly
- if time could stop—just once
- if your birthday was every day of the year, but you got older only once a year
- if your homework did itself
- if you could be in the shoes of someone you most admire, tell what you would do first (as that person)
- if you suddenly found everything you ever lost
- if you could turn back the clock to correct a mistake (or turn the clock ahead so you could see what mistakes you were going to make)
- if you could tell what someone was thinking, in his or her exact words, just by looking at that person
- if you found Aladdin's magic lamp
- if you could change your size or age any time you wanted
- if you really found a pot of gold at the end of a rainbow
- if you could go on a pirate ship
- if you had Superman's x-ray vision
- if all of those funny expressions, such as "all hung up" or "fed up" could be seen happening
- if you remembered exact sentences and paragraphs you read in books and magaz'nes
- if a day's events happened again, only in reverse
- if you had a magic mirror on the wall
- if you could do everything you wanted to, all at one time
- if you owned a pet dragon
- if the colors of birds and trees suddenly changed overnight . . . to purple
- if you had the power to shrink someone you did not like
- if everything was funny
- if you had only three wishes, and only one of them was going to come true

- if your legs were made of rubber
- if you could live under the sea without special equipment
- if you had a part of your life to live over
- if you could learn everything you had to know, instantly, what would be the first thing you did?
- if you had a car that could grow wings to fly over traffic jams and contain all the fuel you would ever need (What would happen if your friends and neighbors ever found out? How would you protect this car?)
- if you could travel faster than the speed of light

LOOKING INTO EDWARD LEAR'S MAGIC WORLD

While the Victorian artist, Edward Lear, is probably best known for his nonsense poems, he also created a magical world of his own, populating it with a variety of make-believe plants, animals and other improbable creatures. For example, there is the elderly Quangle-Wangle in "The Story of the Four Little Children Who Went Round the World." An island these children happened to visit was made up entirely of veal cutlets and chocolate drops. Lear also features unusual creatures, the Jumblies, in a poem about a magical sea voyage. In another short poem, "The Pobble Who Has No Toes," Lear describes the unlikely creature, a Pobble.

To appreciate these works, you should read them (and enjoy Lear's drawings as well) in *The Lear Omnibus* by R.L. Megroz (Thomas Nelson, New York) or in a similar anthology for just about every one of Lear's poems and stories can inspire a wealth of language and craft learning experiences relating to magic and make-believe.

1. Make a new set of magic poems of four or five lines each, beginning as Lear did, with "There was once _____ who (or that) _____." In the first blank, pupils can substitute the name of their own magic island or creature. Encourage pupils to experiment with sounds of words as well as illustrating their inventions.

If each pupil contributes a poem, you might just have enough poems to place in a loose-leaf binder in a book for the class library.

2. Create a new set of adventures for a creature of Lear's not already in a story. Provide this creature with a different background and a new set of friends.

3. Invent "new, improved" magical qualities for Lear's botanical and/or zoological specimens.

4. Make up your own version of a Pobble, Jumblie or four children travelers.

5. Explain how a magic sieve might work. To do this, try getting hold of a real sieve and look it over thoroughly, figuring out what else you can add to it. What kinds of magical properties might it have, either in attachments or invisible qualities?

6. Invent another type of vehicle for Lear's creatures to travel in.

7. Make up your own geography book of magic islands, describing them in your own words and using graph paper to figure out length and distances. Be sure to include locations of unusual features, such as landmarks.

8. Try imagining the effects of sudden growth or shortening of any of Lear's creatures. Then make up a new poem or story that tells what happens and why. Of course, you will also include a different type of problem for this changed creature.

9. Using materials like newspapers, make models of some of Lear's imaginary plants or make up some of your own. On a separate card, write the name of this plant, what it looks like, what it does in ordinary conditions, as well as its reactions to unusual conditions. Also describe the care it requires.

10. Design a story center for a Lear story or poem of your choice. For more details on how to do this, see Chapter 4.

A POTPOURRI OF MAGIC ACTIVITIES

1. Learn how to do a simple trick using coins or cards and teach one of your friends how to do it.

2. Make a list of real and fictional magicians that you would nominate for a "Magicians' Hall of Fame." Then draw pictures of them and write a short description under each.

3. Read the biography of a well-known magician, such as Houdini.

4. Find out why the word "abracadabra" is used. Experiment with its letters, making as many different magic words as you can think of, or print this word over and over until you have made a pattern. In a book about magic and/or magic charms, look for pictures of abracadabra charms.

5. Optical illusions involve tricks played on our eyes. Experiment with a few of these, such as in Figure 9-10. How many different ways can you see the cube?

Figure 9-10

6. Try explaining a scientific phenomenon the way in which primitive people might have viewed it.

7. Describe a magic show, either one you have imagined or actually seen. Include sounds, colors and happenings.

8. Read stories, especially fairy tales, that are about magic and make a list of so-called magic words, items and even lands. What magic thing or things seem to be used the most? Make a graph, showing the least and most popular magic items or words.

9. Compare stories about imaginary witches to those in real life. Were those people really witches? Perhaps you can include your information in a story entitled "The Truth About Witches," or make up a play.

HERE COME THE TRAINS!

At one time or another, most children have been on a train, enjoyed themselves and were surprised to reach another town so quickly. A few children may have been so fascinated with trains that they bought a set of model trains or at least shared their interest with another enthusiast. For these and other reasons, you may wish to enhance a transportation or geography unit with a separate "train center." Your pupils will learn a lot more about trains as a means of transportation and related careers, as well as extend practice of basic skills.

If your city or town has a local train station or subway system, you can probably get a free map of station stops and routes. In some areas, you may even be able to obtain a picture or two of these trains, along with a few timetables. On the other hand, you will also find that the nearest city's train system in your state is a good alternate source of maps and other materials. Beginning with nearby, familiar areas with trains, arrange a field trip with your class.

Start things off by drawing a simple outline of the train system's route on a piece of paper. To do this, use a line to represent the train track and small squares to represent stations. Roughly, your outline will look something like the one in Figure 9-11.

At first, include only necessary details, such as names of stations and nearby towns where the train makes stops—and

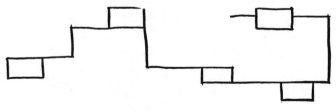

Figure 9-11

simple symbols for any wooded areas, rivers, deserts, landmarks and important buildings. Then develop your sketch on a very large piece of paper, about 30 × 24 inches. If a bulletin board is available, you might consider using its space as a background and pinning or taping cutouts or symbols. Your completed display may look like the one shown in Figure 9-12.

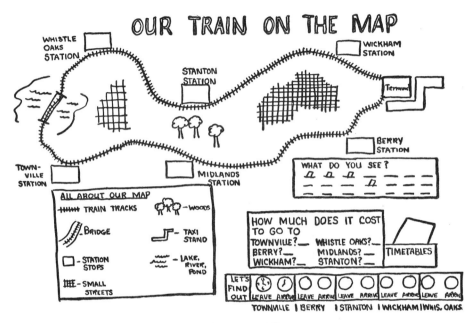

Figure 9-12

Display Suggestions

1. Use children's cutout figures of buildings, people, autos, buses, trucks, trains and signals at various spots.

2. Cut out outlines of stations from pieces of styrofoam, or if you prefer, only doorways, windows and roofs of buildings.

3. Use bits of sponge for leaves on trees. If you are representing the autumn season in this display, combine such colors as yellow, red and brown. Tape or pin various pieces on other areas to represent fallen leaves.

4. Teach children how to read the symbols in the section entitled, "All About Our Map." Let them invent new symbols.

5. If your nearest city does not have a train system that may be included in your display, make one up or use Figure 9-12 as a sample.

6. For clocks in the area marked "Let's Find Out," use paper plates. Turn these plates upside down and draw the clock's face on each of them. Then use a paper fastener to attach hands to each clock. (See Figure 9-13.)

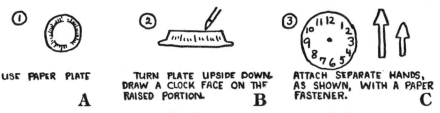

USE PAPER PLATE   TURN PLATE UPSIDE DOWN.   ATTACH SEPARATE HANDS,
                              DRAW A CLOCK FACE ON THE   AS SHOWN, WITH A PAPER
            A   RAISED PORTION.   B   FASTENER.   C

Figure 9-13

7. Make a simple version of the train's timetable, or use an imaginary one, as in Figure 9-14.

MAKE THIS TIMETABLE LESS CONFUSING BY LIMITING IT TO FOUR STATIONS OR LESS.

YOU MIGHT ALSO TRY INCLUDING SEVERAL DIFFERENT SCHEDULES BENEATH THE ROW OF CLOCKS.

Figure 9-14

8. In the section, "What Do You See?," (Figure 9-12) you may have children write names of items they are able to notice directly underneath the caption, cut slits that are large enough to hold children's answers, or attach a separate envelope beneath the caption to hold papers with children's answers.

9. Teach children to use directions when talking about the location of various train stations.

10. In the section "How Much Does It Cost To Go To . . .?" make a separate fares folder, displaying it next to names of station. This folder is simply a large used mailing folder labeled as shown in Figure 9-12.

11. Instead of including details of individual blocks and streets, use faint crayon or magic marker lines to represent such areas. Try crosshatching them, as shown.

12. Build up related reading and math lessons around this train center, using any or all of the suggestions that follow.

Activities for Your Train Center

1. Collect and display copies of artists' paintings of train stations and even trains themselves. One artist worth considering is Edward Hopper.

2. If possible, visit a train station with pupils and ask them to see how many different kinds of activities they see going on inside. For example, an agent might be selling tickets or giving information. Still another worker might be helping to load or unload baggage. A newspaper vendor may be nearby, selling newspapers, magazines and refreshments. Later on, children may make cardboard figures and other models to add to the bulletin board.

3. Make a booklet entitled, "At the Train Station," using as many letters of the alphabet as possible. That is, "c" is for conductor, "e" is for engine, and so on. For a more interesting booklet, try including actual samples of train tickets, timetables, sheets containing new fares notices or holiday changes. Another interesting aspect is what people do as they wait for a train, such as reading newspapers, buying refreshments, sleeping, conversing with fellow passengers or even playing a guitar!

4. Role-play some of the "waiting" activities mentioned in Activity 3.

5. Make maps of the inside of the main terminal, inventing different symbols for the information desk, waiting area, ticket agents and concession stands. Include locations of clocks and information boards, as well as areas and platforms of arriving and departing trains. Give oral directions for reaching a certain platform, for example, using the shortest route possible.

6. Read stories about trains, such as *The Little Engine That Could.* Dramatize favorite stories with plays or puppets.

7. Make up your own story, telling how one of the train stations got its real or imaginary name.

8. Learn what helpers, such as train conductors and baggagemen, do.

9. Draw or paint pictures illustrating what a train station looks like in the spring, summer, autumn and winter. What different activities, sights, sounds and smells take place there?

10. Practice giving directions on how to reach your house or school from a certain station or how to reach a station from a nearby town.

11. Find a poem about trains that seems to include some of the sights your class has seen or heard about involving trains.

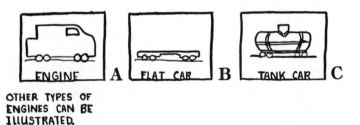

OTHER TYPES OF
ENGINES CAN BE
ILLUSTRATED.

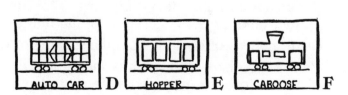

Figure 9-15

12. Practice using sequence by putting cards with pictures of trains on them in order—and describing each in terms of first, second, third and so on. Cut pictures of trains from a magazine or catalog advertisements or try drawing them yourself on 3 × 5-inch cards, using the examples in Figure 9-16 as guides.

Train Activities for Older Pupils

1. Make models of earlier trains, particularly the "Tom Thumb," our first train. Use pictures of these old trains as guides and use scrap materials of your choice for their construction.

2. Collect and analyze ads that try to persuade people to travel by train. What are some of the advantages pupils can think of? Possible disadvantages? Try computing sample expenses from any two given points.

3. Visit a train yard and talk to different workers about their jobs.

4. Collect various train symbols and make up a symbol for your imaginary bulletin board train. (Refer to Figure 9-12.)

5. Read legends of such train heroes as Casey Jones.

6. Have a debate about the use of the train as an energy saver over cars and planes.

7. Find examples of different types of architecture of older train stations in various parts of the country as well as in countries such as England and France. If you happen to live near such an old station, visit it and note as many details as you can in its architecture. Perhaps some pupils will enjoy making drawings of a few details in pen and ink.

8. Design a train station that is pleasing to look at for the present time, or design a station of the future.

9. Learn the role of computers in the running of trains.

10. Make a dictionary of train terms and signals, describing what they look like when possible, and what each one means.

11. Take a "Behind the Scenes" look at various kinds of train careers. Some worthwhile careers to investigate are:

station foreman	brakeman
welder	towerman
yardsmaster	fireman
yard clerk	chef
electrician	stewards
conductor	trainmen
engineer	switchmen
	inspectors

12. Make a booklet, Ripley-style, called, "Would You Believe This About Trains?" In it, include such facts as "Did you know that the first train, *Tom Thumb*, lost its first race to a horse?" as well as lists of songs and stories that feature trains and interesting but little-known facts about various train careers.

Books About Trains

Ault, Phil, *All Aboard, The Story of Passenger Trains in America*, Dodd, Mead, & Co., New York, 1976.

Behans, June, *Train Cargo*, Children's Press, Chicago, 1974.

Buehr, Walter, *Railroads: Today and Yesterday*, G.P. Putnam's Sons, New York, 1957.

Cameron, Elizabeth, *The Big Book of Real Trains*, Grosset & Dunlap, New York, 1976.

Elting, Mary, *Trains at Work*, Harvey House, Irvington-on-Hudson, New York, 1962.

Feldman, Anne, *The Railroad Book: Trains in America*, David McKay Co., New York, 1978.

Mead, Chris, *Careers With a Railroad*, Lerner Publications, Minnesota, 1975.

Rosenfeld, Bernard, *Let's Go to a Freight Yard*, G. P. Putnam's Sons, New York, 1958.

Snow, Paul, *Iron Horse to Diesel*, Whitman Pub. Co., Wisconsin, 1961.

STONEHENGE AS AN ANCIENT MYSTERY

For the most part, Stonehenge still remains a mystery to scientists, archaeologists and laypersons alike. Many important questions are still unanswered. Why was Stonehenge really built? What was the real purpose of the Aubrey stones? Was Stonehenge intended as an astronomical observatory, or not? In spite of much recently uncovered information, the answers to a few theories are unknown, and probably will remain so for some time. But why try to figure out Stonehenge in the first place? What about other similar henge monuments in England and a portion of western Europe? True, only a part of Stonehenge is actually standing. However, the amount of other henges' existing remains seems less than those of Stonehenge, for the most part. Perhaps these mysteries may yield more answers . . .

In the meantime, Stonehenge as an ancient mystery appeals to adults and children as well. Besides, it is a good topic you can use in the classroom in just about any curriculum area; archaeology, art, social studies and language arts. To begin, you may wish to borrow or display books about archaeology, including Stonehenge, in the class library. Or use a simple, attractive bulletin board to motivate children. (See examples which follow.) Still another way is reading a legend about Stonehenge to your class, or even having children pretend to take an archaeological picture, description or dialogue tour of Stonehenge.

Figure 9-16

Suggestions For Making Stonehenge Bulletin Boards

Bulletin Board # 1—"Let's Focus on Stonehenge"

1. Instead of drawing magic marker lines to represent Stonehenge, try substituting construction paper cutouts for various stones. For lighter stones, use gray, beige or light yellow construction paper. For darker stones and shadows, experiment with darker hues of gray, blue, maroon, purple or even black. Or have one of your more artistic pupils make a large drawing from a photograph of Stonehenge.

2. Experiment with different types of lettering. Figure 9-16 shows one of many possible ways. You might decide to use poster paints or pieces of rope or cardboard to spell "Stonehenge."

3. Attach individual pictures of different views of Stonehenge down opposite sides of the bulletin board, as shown in Figure 9-17. Or use individual, original bookcovers made by children.

4. Substitute smaller pictures by placing them around and beneath the caption, "Let's Focus on Stonehenge."

Figure 9-17

Bulletin Board # 2—Read About "The Mystery of Stonehenge."

1. Use a dark, thin magic marker line for the words, "Read About" and a heavier, squiggly line for the book title, "The Mystery of Stonehenge," as shown in the illustration in Figure 9-18.

Figure 9-18

2. Fold a large piece of oaktag or other heavy paper in half, glue a picture of Stonehenge directly beneath the title, and you have an "instant" bulletin board.

3. Or eliminate the book completely and only include "The Mystery of Stonehenge" along with a larger picture of Stonehenge directly underneath.

4. Place caption at the top and various bookcovers made by the class directly underneath.

A List of Helpful Books About Stonehenge and Other Mysteries for Teachers and Children

Atkinson, R.J.C., *Stonehenge,* Hamish, Hamilton, London.

Cusack, Michael J., *Is There a Bermuda Triangle? Science and Sea Mysteries,* Julius Messner, New York, 1976.

Gallagher, I.J., *The Case of the Ancient Astronauts,* Raintree Children's Books, Milwaukee, 1977.

Hadingham, Evan, *Circles and Standing Stones,* Anchor Press/ Doubleday, Garden City, New York, 1976.

Hawkins, Gerald S., *Stonehenge Decoded,* Doubleday & Co., New York, 1965.

Layrock, George, *Islands and Their Mysteries,* Four Winds Press, New York, 1977.

Stover, Leon and Kraig, Bruce, *Stonehenge: the Indo-European Heritage,* Nelson-Hall, Chicago, 1978.

Ward, Anne, *Adventures in Archaeology,* Larouse & Co., New York, 1977.

Wood, John, *Sun, Moon, and Standing Stones,* Oxford University Press, New York, 1978.

Activities for Stonehenge as an Ancient Mystery

1. Find out the meaning of words such as "henge," "megalith" and "Stonehenge." Include these words in a separate glossary/folder that children can illustrate.

2. Make small pictures representing symbols of other henges and place them on a large map of Great Britain.

3. The lever was used to raise large stones. Use a ruler as a lever to lift a child's block or a small book. Find pictures of other kinds of levers and how they operate.

4. Make a large timeline of the building of Stonehenge by illustrating and describing Stonehenge I, II and III. You will find a useful description in Stover and Kraig's book, *Stonehenge: the Indo-European Heritage*. An example is shown in Figure 9-19.

INCLUDE INFORMATION ABOUT THE AGRICULTURAL AND POLITICAL ACTIVITIES THAT OCCURRED IN EACH STAGE.

Figure 9-19

5. Try pretending that Stonehenge was actually figured out and write about what happens from this time on. In addition to an eye-catching newspaper headline and some fictitious date, you will have to invent the type of evidence found (was it bones, stone carvings, etc.?) and what such discoveries mean. Take the role of a newspaper reporter, a feature writer or an archaeologist, and include what you know in a series of newspaper or magazine articles.

6. Collect as many theories as possible associated with Stonehenge. Make up your own ideas as to the why and how of Stonehenge using some of the information you have. Then represent various authorities in a role-playing situation, justifying a certain theory to your peers and convincing those peers that you are right.

7. Think of ways to help prevent the monument from falling down and being completely ruined. Take into consideration the heavy traffic that rumbles past the monument every day as well as large daily crowds of tourists. If possible, get a map of this area of England from a book about this monument.

8. Read legends associated with Stonehenge, and either dramatize them or use them to make up your own.

9. Make individual postcards of Stonehenge and think of messages you can use to write on the back.

10. Make a model of Stonehenge, using clay.

11. Compare pictures showing various perspectives of Stonehenge—bird's-eye view, view from a plane, eye level and from an ant's view. Then use each of these views to write and even draw "A Portrait of Stonehenge."

12. Write each new word you've learned about Stonehenge on separate 3 × 5-inch cards. Place all of these cards in an open box lid. Individual players may win a certain number of points by:

    (a) reading each word correctly, or

    (b) giving an accurate description of the word.

    Words may include any or all of the following: megalith, Beaker people, Windmill Hill people, Wessex farmers, henge, neolithic, Aubrey Holes, Heel Stone, lintel, menhir, Druids, sarsen circle, trilithon, Slaughter Stone, Station Stones, Avebury, barrows, Salisbury Plain, double bluestone circle.

13. Use Stonehenge as the background for a short science fiction story.

THE EXCITING WORLD OF TELEVISION: A "BEHIND THE SCENES" LOOK

Television has much to offer in the way of entertainment. But what happens "behind the scenes" is just as fascinating as turning on the TV set and seeing a picture suddenly appear on the screen. For one thing, a number of people are involved—producers, writers and directors, to name a few. Then many specialized tasks have to be done before a single program can be televised. This is true of situation comedies as well as news programs. Everyone must work together, for deadlines must also be met. In addition to these so-called "hidden agendas," television involves related aspects of commercials, reviews and ratings.

As interesting as all of these aspects are, they are only a part of the reason why television is such a good topic in the classroom. It provides children with various opportunities to think and judge, read, write, review and learn about some new careers. In addition to plenty of activities in the language arts, a television topic involves curriculum areas such as social studies, math, science, and the arts. Moreover, you will find that such a topic can be adapted to just about any grade level. You may wish to use the following activities "as is," or change them to suit the needs of younger children.

1. To become more familiar with a television studio, your class can probably visit one, or at least write for information. Use the following addresses:

   WCBS—TV
   51 West 52nd St.
   New York, New York

   WABC Television Station
   1330 Ave. of the Americas
   New York, New York

   WNBC—Television Station
   30 Rockefeller Plaza
   New York, New York

   Find pictures or descriptions of an interior of a TV studio in children's books about TV, and use them as guides in making a diorama with pipe cleaner figures. In this case, your pupils will find that a large cardboard carton often is most effective. They should prepare this box, using the pictures and directions in Figure 9-20 as a guide.

2. Look for information about television-related careers, such as writer, reporter, film editor, editor, cameraperson, anchorperson, production assistant, technical director, makeup artist, director, view controller, and video operator. You will find books such as Edward Stoddard's *The First Book of Television* (Franklin Watts, New York) and Barbara Steinberg's *Who Puts the News*

on Television? (Random House, New York, 1976) very helpful. Then have your students make a booklet of careers that they found interesting. Or make pipe cleaner figures of various TV people, along with tools of their professions. Then place each figure on a clay, cardboard, or spool stand, and write a short description of his specialty on it. (See Figure 9-21.)

A

PLACE THE CARTON SO THAT ITS OPEN SIDE IS UP. THEN CUT AWAY ONE ENTIRE FRONT PANEL AS SHOWN BY THE BROKEN LINES.

B

THEN TURN THE CARTON UNTIL ITS OPPOSITE PANEL FACES YOU. ON THIS SIDE, MAKE 5 EVENLY-SPACED ROWS OF BROKEN LINES, ABOUT 2"-3" APART. TRY TO KEEP EACH ROW AS EVEN AS POSSIBLE. CUT ALONG THE HEAVY LINE AND ALONG THE BOTTOM.

C

FOLD THE REMAINING ROWS OF BROKEN LINES, SO THAT EACH SIDE LOOKS LIKE THE PICTURE IN 3B.

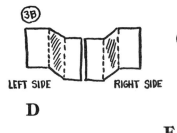

LEFT SIDE   RIGHT SIDE

D

E

ATTACH THE OPEN SIDES WITH A PIECE OF ADHESIVE TAPE AS SHOWN. THIS DIAGRAM SHOWS HOW THE BACK OF YOUR "STUDIO" WILL LOOK.

F

PLACE THE BOTTOM OF THE CARTON ON A LARGE PIECE OF STIFF CARD-BOARD SO THAT THE WHOLE FLOOR IS COMPLETE. ADD DETAILS BY PAINT-ING AND WITH SEPARATE FIGURES.

Figure 9-20

MATCH STICK

OF COURSE, YOU CAN MAKE CONSTRUCTION PAPER CLOTHES AND FEATURES FOR YOUR FIGURE

USE A SPOOL AS A CHAIR.

MATCH BOX

TELEVISION WRITER

Figure 9-21

3. To learn more about what goes on "behind the scenes," collect articles about a TV star or favorite newsperson, if available.

4. Try visiting a real television studio.

5. Have each child take part in writing a short play that may be shown on television and simulating a small-scale production of it. That is, ask volunteers to role-play editors, directors, producers and others. Then have other children act as reviewers and rate the show accordingly. Draw up a list of rating standards, such as general audience appeal, scenery, dialogue, props and acting.

6. Try simulating an imaginary game show, using facts from class work for the questions and answers. You might try rating this show. To do this, revise rating standards mentioned above to include length of show, contestants' behavior, interest, and so on.

7. Collect cartoons from newspapers and magazines involving people and television.

8. The next time you watch a television show, make up a checklist of items that should be considered in giving the show a "good" or "bad" rating. Begin with one of your favorite television programs.

9. Try taking a class poll of popular and favorite television programs. What do you think makes them so popular?

10. Make a graph of various aspects of television, such as how long commercials take, what types of programs seem to be featured at certain times, or the types of jobs and professions represented in popular shows.

11. In a recent *TV Guide,* find an article that interests you and write a report of it. Or use suggestions for ways to tell about a book in Chapter 4.

12. Learn more about how cameras work by making a pinhole camera from a small cardboard box. You can find directions for such cameras in children's books about photography or physics.

13. Make a chart illustrating how *not* to use television. For example, do not try repairing a TV set yourself, and during a thunderstorm unplug the TV set.

14. In color television, signals stand for the colors red, green and blue. Experiment with these colors using flashlights covered with colored cellophane. Have students cross the colored beams of light, proving that any color can be made just by using these three.

15. Tell the story of television by making a short moving picture show. First make a list of landmark dates in the development of television on a piece of paper, beginning with William Crookes' discovery of the cathode-ray tube in 1878. You will find a more detailed story in Stoddard's *The First Book of Television* (Franklin Watts, New York). Or look in other children's books about television.

    Then divide a strip of wrapping paper, about 36-40 inches long and 5 inches wide in the number of desired sections, as shown in Figure 9-22, or tape separate pieces of 5 × 6-inch paper in one long strip. Be sure to allow one section of your strip for a title, such as "The Story of Television" and a last section with the words, "The End."

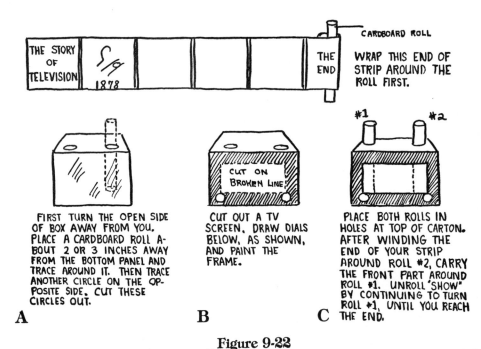

THE STORY OF TELEVISION   1878   THE END

CARDBOARD ROLL

WRAP THIS END OF STRIP AROUND THE ROLL FIRST.

A FIRST TURN THE OPEN SIDE OF BOX AWAY FROM YOU. PLACE A CARDBOARD ROLL ABOUT 2 OR 3 INCHES AWAY FROM THE BOTTOM PANEL AND TRACE AROUND IT. THEN TRACE ANOTHER CIRCLE ON THE OPPOSITE SIDE. CUT THESE CIRCLES OUT.

B CUT OUT A TV SCREEN. DRAW DIALS BELOW, AS SHOWN, AND PAINT THE FRAME.

CUT ON BROKEN LINE

C #1 #2 PLACE BOTH ROLLS IN HOLES AT TOP OF CARTON. AFTER WINDING THE END OF YOUR STRIP AROUND ROLL #2, CARRY THE FRONT PART AROUND ROLL #1. UNROLL 'SHOW' BY CONTINUING TO TURN ROLL #1, UNTIL YOU REACH THE END.

Figure 9-22

Beginning with the earliest date, around 1878, continue on to more recent times and draw or paste a picture of some aspect of TV's history in each section. Then wind the last sections of your strip around a cardboard roll (from aluminum foil, wax paper, etc.). For added effectiveness, try making a cardboard carton look like a television set, as shown in Figures 9-22A, B and C.

10

PRACTICAL TESTING METHODS THAT MEASURE PROGRESS

The next time you give a test, try noticing how individual children react. You will probably find that some children seem to change their answers constantly. Other pupils write at a steady pace; some take a few extra minutes to think of that correct answer; while some merely make a wild guess. Occasionally, a few children may even decide that the test is too difficult and give up altogether. These are typical reactions in many classrooms. Learn to use them!

As you check and grade test papers, take another look at answers given by your average and slower pupils in particular. The chances are good that you can help many of those children improve their scores and even their attitudes toward test taking in general.

This does not mean that you must coach pupils with the right answers or offer strong hints as to what those answers might be during the test. Far from it! Rather, you should realize that test taking *is* an art, and the way in which questions are answered matters just as much as the type of answers given. But more about this in the following sections.

GUIDELINES TO AID PUPILS IN TEST-TAKING

Before an upcoming test, many pupils are likely to feel anxious and perhaps somewhat frightened. By recalling your own feelings just before a big test, you already have an idea of children's anxiety. Some of this anxiety helps test performance, of course. But many times, this anxiety only hinders progress, and can be due to any or all of the following:

1. *Poor study techniques.* Remember that even brighter students hesitate in asking questions and clearing up confusion. Many children tend to procrastinate in reviewing their notes, for they assume that they know the material. More likely, these pupils have a vague idea of their notes. Finally, they may be unwilling or unable to study it until details are mastered.

2. *Reading difficulties* may tempt a child to guess haphazardly and lower his or her chances for a better grade. Still, some pupils may not interpret direction words in a test correctly. For example, words like "Explain," "List," or "Outline" may be a source of much confusion to pupils. Various spelling words do sound alike, yet have different meanings—sea, see; their, there; and to, two, and too. In helping these children, try to avoid pronouncing such words consecutively in a spelling test. Or better yet, help children distinguish these words by using them in distinctive sentences.

   Also, a test's appearance may contribute other reading problems. Have you noticed, for example, how much easier it is to read a printed test than one that has been handwritten? And how frustrating some of those mimeographed tests are to read? Their print is sometimes too light or blotchy. If you must use such tests, check each sheet before distributing them to the class.

   Finally, you may also find that having a short review of certain direction words is very helpful. For example, do your pupils know the difference between "define" and "name," "explain" and "compare," "add" and "subtract," and "divide" and "multiply"? In addition to reviewing these terms, use these words in games and even in practice tests.

3. *The child's initial panic as tests are being given out.* Regardless of how well a child has studied, or how confident he or she appears, that child may still experience

some momentary panic—and this may affect his or her performance.

4. *A child may not know HOW to take a test.* Often, test directions and questions are read too fast in efforts to respond. For example, what a pupil *thinks* he reads and what is actually in the question may be two different things. The result is usually a wrong answer and a lower score than the pupil deserves Some children spend all of their time on two or three questions, losing out on credit that they may have earned. Again, a lower score is the result.

In the long run, it may be possible that certain kinds of questions present more problems to some children than others.

a. *Fill-ins.* There is nothing the matter with fill-ins. However, fill-in questions *can* be tricky. You may have a definite word in mind, only to find that a child has supplied an equivalent, correct answer. Usually, this problem can be solved by giving full or partial credit, depending on how close that answer is.

b. *Multiple-choice.* In these questions, it is quite easy to overlook two choices that are different in the most subtle way. For all the child knows, both choices may be correct. So he takes a guess and chooses one, running a higher risk of getting an incorrect answer. Probably the best way of avoiding these circumstances is reading the test questions again, from a child's point of view.

c. *Essay.* These questions mean problems for some students because of the confusion in interpreting direction words mentioned above. Again, some pupils may feel overwhelmed by these questions because they do not know how to begin answering them. In addition to helping children understand direction words, take some time out to teach them how to make a very simple outline.

HOW TO HELP PUPILS BEFORE A TEST

1. Having made up your own test, set it aside for a day or two. Then read it again, using the following checklist.

Checklist for Evaluating Your Own Tests

Have I reviewed my objectives for this test? In each question, have I:

- thought of (and included) any new, but good questions
- thought of changing or checking questions for clarity.
    - a. *Fill-ins.* Revised so that the desired answer can be provided with less confusion? Allowed enough leeway to grant credit for close answers?
    - b. *Multiple-choice.* Checked for choices that sound too much the same?
    - c. *Essay.* Used terms that pupils will most likely understand? Is it a clear question?
- thought how an average, bright or slower child might interpret individual test items? And what about children who tend to panic, regardless of their abilities? (You can usually tell by the kinds of wrong answers to so-called "easy questions.")
- recalled the kinds of tests that pupils responded especially well to, or seemed to have the most difficulty with for reasons other than not studying?
- included a variety of types of questions whenever possible?
- remembered to include one or two questions that can be answered by all pupils? (A little motivation often goes a long way!)
- found out approximately how much time my class will need to complete this test?

2. Teach, or review with pupils, various study techniques. For example, you might:

- show the class how to rephrase key concepts or shorten lengthy notes by paring unnecessary words such as "and," "the," "are," "those." In other words, is it possible to use three or four important words instead of eight or ten? Sometimes, phrases may be used in place of complete sentences. Or a small picture might be included in place of words.

- Help pupils see that facts are related. In math, for instance, knowing that 8×9 equals the same answer as 9×8 can help many children.

- Show your pupils different ways to record their notes for easier studying later on. Rewriting notes on 3×5-inch cards and carrying them around is one possible way, but these cards are easily lost or misplaced. How about rewriting a shortened version of these notes on separate pieces of 5×7-inch paper, and stapling them together at one end to make a miniature booklet? This booklet may be folded in half, making it easy for pupils to place notes in pockets and pocketbooks.

  As children rewrite their notes, suggest that they print, or substitute pictures for words, for a different set of notes.

  Whether pupils revise their notes or not, they should be encouraged to use odd moments to look these notes over—such as during the time spent in waiting for buses or trains, or even during a longer-than-usual TV commercial!

- Have children begin revising their notes into shorter versions about a week or so before the test. By doing this, pupils will have to review their material in different ways. For example, they may have to restate this information in their own words.

- If possible, ask children to summarize their notes orally for parents or other family members.

- Try reassuring children that there is nothing wrong about feeling anxious before a test. Nearly everyone who takes a test feels concerned about his or her performance, or ought to.

- Try planning to have a short review a day or so before the test. Remind pupils that the test will include material they have studied. This is also a good time for clearing up any confusing words, ideas and concepts.

HELPS TO MAKE TESTING EASIER

In addition to reminding pupils about bringing extra pens or pencils, being neat and working carefully, you can encourage them to try such suggestions as:

1. Unless otherwise directed, children should take a moment or two to look at the whole test. They may use this time to understand directions better. Then have them take one deep breath before doing the test.

2. After looking at the test, pupils may try answering easier questions *first*. Of course, this may vary from pupil to pupil. Some may prefer tackling questions carrying the most credit before attempting equally easy questions carrying less credit. Each child will have to decide what way is best for him or her.

3. Having decided upon which question to answer first, the child should read carefully to know exactly what is being called for. Nothing should be written down until the child is sure. Once the question is clear, it can be answered accordingly.

4. While a reasonable amount of time should be allowed for each question, pupils can budget their time so as to be able to answer each item. Certain types of items, such as essay questions, usually require more thinking time than multiple-choice questions.

   In any case, multiple-choice questions are more easily answered if pupils can eliminate a choice that is obviously wrong. If a child is uncertain about a choice, he or she should first answer it in pencil and return to it later.

5. Instead of quickly changing answers, children should try completing the test first, and then returning to the miss-

ing iems. If the question seems too difficult, then a careful guess may be made.

To answer essay questions, children should write their thoughts in order, if possible, on a piece of scrap paper instead of making a detailed outline.

6. Sometimes, let children know what you are looking for as you score their test. Mention neatness, for one, and following directions as another.

7. Let your pupils know beforehand about how much time they may have for the test and encourage them to budget this time accordingly. Try to avoid writing the remaining minutes on the board at short intervals, if possible. This practice is often very distracting to pupils.

ONE WAY TO LEARN HOW TO TAKE A TEST

Next to reading and remembering, practicing a given skill is probably the best way to learn it. In taking a test, for example, children must use various skills—budgeting their time well, reading and understanding directions, and answering different types of questions. You can often explain these skills to your class. Better yet, you will want to provide opportunities for children to practice such skills. To do this, you will need tests.

One way to get these tests is by collecting various practice tests from outdated texts, workbooks and similar materials. Ideally, you should have a test for each child in your class, or at least half of your class. Perhaps a similar practice test can be found for the other pupils. As you probably realize, getting and collecting these tests often takes a long time, even if you can persuade other teachers to save their old tests for you.

On the other hand, you will find that making up your own test is not as difficult as it sounds. For its length, types of questions and even subject matter can vary widely. It can also be based on one of those old commercial tests, if you prefer. Or this practice test can be fun, with different questions about certain television programs, current pupil interests, past and upcoming holidays, and so on. In such a test, children will make good use of other skills, such as reading, reasoning and writing.

To make up one practice test, choose a suitable category for the grade level of your pupils, and finally narrow it down to a more defined topic. For example, you may choose "spring" as a category and the circus as a topic. While this topic may be narrowed down further, it still offers possibilities for a very short practice test, such as the one shown below:

PRACTICE TEST

At the Circus

I. *Directions.* Write the correct word in each sentence.

1. One food that monkeys and elephants both enjoy is <u>(peanuts)</u>.

2. The <u>(ringmaster)</u> tells you what act will be on next.

3. The clown's funny tricks make us <u>(laugh)</u>.

II. *Directions.* Draw a circle around the letter of the best answer.

1. A person who performs with wild animals is a(n)
   a. tight-rope walker.
   b. ringmaster.
   c. animal tamer.

2. Most of the time, the circus comes to town in the
   a. winter.
   b. spring.
   c. fall.

3. The animals do tricks because they are
   a. trained.
   b. paid.
   c. fooled.

4. The clown's tricycle has
   a. 4 wheels.
   b. 1 wheel.
   c. 3 wheels.

After obtaining or making up a short practice test, try simulating test conditions. Tell your pupils that they are going to practice taking a test. Add other details about this simulation, such as the test topic, when it will be given and reassure children that it will not be hard.

On the day of the test, simulate actual test conditions. Have pupils follow usual seating and marking procedures. Remind children that you expect them to act as though they were taking a real test. At the end of this test, have pupils turn in papers the usual way. Or, vary this procedure—perhaps children can use a code letter or number instead of their own names and mark each other's papers.

After reviewing answers to these tests, take some time to ask children what types of questions they found easiest or hardest to do (fill-ins? multiple-choice? essay?) and why. Let children know that they will be able to improve their test-taking skills in upcoming practice sessions.

In these later sessions (about one session every two or three weeks or so), you will be able to get much done. You will be able to help more children gain confidence in themselves as they practice taking tests, as well as help them cope with longer tests, improve certain reading or math skills, understand other direction words and learn more. By all means, add elements of fun to these tests—a humorous line, a picture, an interesting fact or question. All of these things will motivate children to do their best and feel less anxious about the idea of taking a test.

WHAT A TEST IS—AND ISN'T

At some time, many pupils will again be taking tests in order to be admitted to college or obtain employment. These tests and similar ones are among various criteria used in measuring many abilities. Such tests are often useful guides. On a less positive level, tests are sometimes used as the only method of judging individuals and most of all, relied upon to compare scores of separate groups rather than measure or compare a person's present performance with his or her previous one. This would almost seem that when tests are good, they are very good, and when they are bad, they are really terrible. There are many disagreements on just what makes one test good and another bad. Controversy about this and other aspects of testing is likely to continue for some time.

When it comes down to the test itself, most people immediately think of the paper and pencil type. In many cases, this is true. Just about all of the standard tests and certainly many teacher-made tests do require written answers. But there are other ways to evaluate children, such as oral and performance-type tests. In the classroom, this usually means that you, as a teacher, are constantly evaluating children with these tests and other means. To help make that evaluation more effective, you should consider having children evaluate themselves in other ways. The next section describes some of these ways.

WAYS TO HELP THEM EVALUATE THEMSELVES

Allowing children to evaluate themselves is an effective way to increase their mastery of certain concepts. It can also aid them in memorizing such material as number facts. By checking their progress, children will be motivated to continue any good work or improve areas that need work. You will also find this self-evaluation helpful to use in addition to results of written tests. Some ways to provide pupils with the means to test themselves are shown below. Of course, all of these ways can be varied and adapted to meet the needs of all children.

Examples of Math Self-Evaluation Aids

1. *Opposite drill cards,* such as those shown in Figure 10-1.
2. *Laminated word cards.* These cards include blank spaces and separate answer pieces.

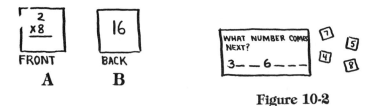

FRONT   BACK

A   B

Figure 10-2

3. *Box lid math.* Cut slits as shown in Figure 10-3 and write problems you wish to have pupils study. Underneath each lid, write the answer. To use, child lifts up flap and "checks" his answer.

4. *Math strips.* (See Figure 10-4.)

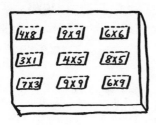

Figure 10-3

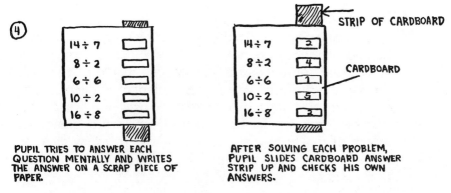

PUPIL TRIES TO ANSWER EACH QUESTION MENTALLY AND WRITES THE ANSWER ON A SCRAP PIECE OF PAPER.

AFTER SOLVING EACH PROBLEM, PUPIL SLIDES CARDBOARD ANSWER STRIP UP AND CHECKS HIS OWN ANSWERS.

Figure 10-4

Examples of Language Self-Evaluation Helps

1. *Flip spelling cards.* (See Figure 10-5.)
2. *Word strips.* (See Figure 10-6.)

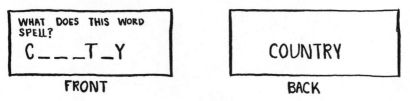

Figure 10-5

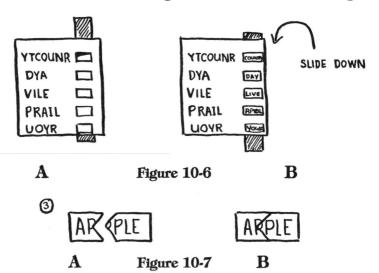

A   **Figure 10-6**   **B**

A   **Figure 10-7**   **B**

3. *Fractured words.* (See Figure 10-7.)

4. *Make-a-Sentence.* To make this self-test, you will need a box lid and slips of paper, about 2 × 4 inches. First, write completed sentences directly on the inside of the box lid. Then write each word of a sentence on each slip of paper (or cardboard, if you wish). To use, pupil reads the first sentence in the box lid and uses word pieces to match or make up a similar sentence. You may also include separate slips of paper or cardboard with punctuation marks.

Figure 10-8

INDEX

WIDENER COLLEGE WOLFGRAM LIBRARY CHESTER, PA.

DATE DUE

OCT 2 8 1981			
FEB 2 3 1983			
OCT 0 2 1985			
FEB 1 9 1986			
AUG 1 0 1988			
DEC 1 4 1988			
DEC 1 3 1989			
MAY MAR 1994 2004			

DEMCO 38-297